MW01413024

My Story, Your Story
Devotions When Life Really Stinks!

A Collection of Life's Trials by Women and How Faith Brought Them through the Fire.

Collected by

Andrea Leffew

WESTBOW PRESS
A DIVISION OF THOMAS NELSON
& ZONDERVAN

Copyright © 2014 Andrea Leffew.

All rights reserved. No part of this book may be used or reproduced by any means, graphic, electronic, or mechanical, including photocopying, recording, taping or by any information storage retrieval system without the written permission of the publisher except in the case of brief quotations embodied in critical articles and reviews.

WestBow Press books may be ordered through booksellers or by contacting:

WestBow Press
A Division of Thomas Nelson & Zondervan
1663 Liberty Drive
Bloomington, IN 47403
www.westbowpress.com
1 (866) 928-1240

Because of the dynamic nature of the Internet, any web addresses or links contained in this book may have changed since publication and may no longer be valid. The views expressed in this work are solely those of the author and do not necessarily reflect the views of the publisher, and the publisher hereby disclaims any responsibility for them.

Any people depicted in stock imagery provided by Thinkstock are models, and such images are being used for illustrative purposes only. Certain stock imagery © Thinkstock.

Scripture taken from the Holy Bible, NEW INTERNATIONAL VERSION®. Copyright © 1973, 1978, 1984 by Biblica, Inc. All rights reserved worldwide. Used by permission. NEW INTERNATIONAL VERSION® and NIV® are registered trademarks of Biblica, Inc. Use of either trademark for the offering of goods or services requires the prior written consent of Biblica US, Inc.

ISBN: 978-1-4908-5704-6 (sc)
ISBN: 978-1-4908-5706-0 (hc)
ISBN: 978-1-4908-5705-3 (e)

Library of Congress Control Number: 2014918848

Printed in the United States of America.

WestBow Press rev. date: 12/19/2014

For my husband who has put up with me with love and my daughters who have shown grace, courage and strength through their daily trials

Acknowledgment

"Fear not, for I have redeemed you; you are mine. When you pass through the waters, I will be with you; and when you pass through the rivers, they will not sweep over you. When you walk through the fire, you will not be burned; the flames will not set you ablaze."

Isaiah 43:2

This devotional book is written from the hearts of women I know and women I do not know. I asked them to imagine they were talking to a friend over coffee and that her friend just revealed she was in the midst of a trial, a trial they themselves had once walked through. I asked them to be honest with the feelings they had going through that trial. I asked them to write their pain, hurt, or mistakes of that time. And then how their faith brought them through the flames.

These brave women responded in an amazing way. They had the courage to open areas of their hearts that have been hidden. Old wounds were reopened, truths were found, hidden fears of embarrassment and shame were brought to light. I was told by some of these ladies that they wrote through the tears in their eyes. Others said that it was very difficult to go back to that time, but that it was also healing. But they all said that if what they went through could be helpful to someone else, it was worth it.

I hope the words of these brave women will speak blessings into your life. Maybe you will find in this devotional a story just like yours or maybe read one that brings the same feelings to your heart. Some of the names have been changed at the request of the ladies. You will find different writing styles, as different as the trials and the women who wrote them.

I want to thank these women for their courage and willingness to step out to their comfort zone and making this devotional possible.

Andrea

Preface

> *"Do not cast me from your presence or take your Holy Spirit from me. Restore to me the joy of your salvation and grant me a willing spirit, to sustain me."*
>
> Psalm 51:11-12

I was in the midst of an ugly divorce in 1999. I was struggling not to slash his tires or throw eggs at her house. I did not want to go through this divorce and be ashamed of how I behaved. I wanted to be a godly woman. So I went to the local Christian bookstore looking for some encouragement or guidance. I was under so much stress during that time, that I knew I could only concentrate enough on something short, like a devotional book.

The nice lady led me to the devotion section. Everything was soft, calm, butterflies, pastels and daisies. I was ANGRY, I was HURT, I was JAGGED, I was BLACK and RED not cream and pink! I didn't see any books that related to my pain. The words to this book came to my mind at that moment!

For 17 years I have had this book in my heart, but I was afraid to put myself out in public and put this book together. I was even afraid to tell anyone about this idea, due to fear of being ridiculed or being a failure. Recently, I had been feeling that

I was not putting God first in my life and had felt that I was blocking His words to me. I started praying to hear the Holy Spirit again and to show me how I was being disobedient to Him. The name of the book came to my heart again. I knew I had to step out of myself and do this devotion. I called my husband, crying I told him what I needed to do. We prayed. I started typing emails to women and fought my fear of letting them down the whole time.

So here it is. I pray it will meet you where you are. These devotions were written by women struggling with real life trials and how they survive. I hope one of these devotions will give you hope and strength to know there is peace in your trial. Christ is with you.

Andrea
www.MyStoryYourStory2.com.

To quickly find a specific topic, go to the **Subject Index** on page 121.

My Story 1

"In this you greatly rejoice, though now for a little while you may have had to suffer grief in all kinds of trials. These have come so that your faith-of greater worth than gold, which perishes even though refined by fire-may be proved genuine and may result in praise, glory and honor when Jesus Christ is revealed."

1 Peter 1:6-7

I woke up shaking. I had been praying to know what to do. I knew divorce is wrong, but I also knew this marriage was wrong in so many ways. I had enough reasons for divorcing him by the world's standards, but not by Gods. My proverbial "line in the sand" was physical abuse and adultery. I thought that verbal and mental abuse was ok! We had tried counseling with no change and always the same response from him; "that it was my fault".

I had resolved myself to stay in the marriage, even if it meant a loveless and abusive life. But God gave me my 'line in the sand'! One day, I had dropped the girls off at school. My hands started to shake on the steering wheel and instead of heading to work I headed to the hotel he was staying at with his visiting mother. In the parking lot, I saw the company van that I had seen the 'HER' in just the other day. I became suddenly calm. I casually walked into the hotel lobby, and asked for his room. The clerk wouldn't give me the number, but I saw it on the computer screen. I walked up the stairs to his room, I passed a maid and told her I had forgotten my key and asked if she would open the door for me.

The security latch was on, so I stuck my foot in the door jamb to keep the door open a few inches. I called his name (the poor maid quietly disappeared!). There was noise and commotion going on in the room. I called out again, this time I could hear the window opening and some more rustling around. He was seeing if he could jump out the window, too bad the room was on the second floor.

Finally, after what seemed like hours, he opened the door. There they stood, one bed messed up, and the other never touched. Both of them trying to tell me nothing happened. I guess I looked that stupid to them! That whole morning I had felt the Holy Spirit guiding me, but it was the devil that I gave into at that moment. I went up to my husband and kicked him HARD in the groin. I went over to her, slapped her in the face and called her a few names! That was the most I let the devil have control over me.

The first stop was an urgent care clinic to be tested for any STDs. I then called to make an appointment to have an alarm system put in my home. I finally went to an attorney and started filing those horrible divorce papers. Sitting there filling out the divorce forms was the worst moment of the day. Seeing the words on paper was the final heartbeat of my marriage. My marriage was dead. The dreams I had for my future as his wife were dead. Holidays and family celebrations were now dead. It was there at the attorney's office with clipboard and pen in hand that I finally broke down and cried.

We had a very ugly divorce. He had said that if I divorced him, he would make my life miserable. At times I felt he had succeeded with his threat. But God had placed people in my life to help me and my daughters. I joined a divorce support group and was given the best advice from the moderator. He said that when I think about doing something hateful to my ex to remember that "When I die, I will be standing in front of God. God will not be there asking me about my ex, He will want to know what I did".

I had gone through the fires of abuse and divorce but it was because of this pain, I had learned to read the Bible and trust the Lord. I learned scriptures and clung to them as I headed to court again and again for custody battles. I asked and accepted forgiveness from God when I did and said things I shouldn't have during the divorce. I cried over the Psalms when I could not sleep at night, feeling alone and weak. I learned to trust others, remove my pride, and ask for help. But more importantly, I learned above all things to raise my hands up, in all circumstances, in praise to God!!

Anonymous

My Story 2

"For I am convinced that neither death nor life, neither angels nor demons, neither the present nor the future, nor any powers, neither height nor depth, nor anything else in all creation, will be able to separate us from the love of God that is in Christ Jesus our Lord."

Romans 8:38-39

My son had a genetic disease called Cystic Fibrosis (CF). He had an exceptionally bad case, and after being on oxygen for a solid two years, and waiting patiently for a lung transplant, he lost his battle for life at the age of twelve.

A scene that is permanently emblazoned on my memory is when Ryan was in his last few hours of life. My brother-in-law, Tom, was singing this sweet song to Ryan, as he drifted in and out of sleep: "Jesus, Jesus, Jesus….There's just something about that name. Master, Savior, Jesus, like the fragrance after the rain…" It was in that moment that Ryan mumbled something that got our attention. Uncle Tom asked Ryan what he had just said. Ryan quietly responded, "I saw Jesus, and I'm going with Him". There was no fear, no anxiousness, only peace. It was also a gift from my God! He allowed us the same peace that he gave to Ryan.

The knowledge that Ryan did indeed see his Savior and was going with Him! It's been one of the sweet gifts God has given to me as Ryan's mother. The assurance that God is real, that Heaven is real, and that I will get to see my sweet boy again!

Annette

My Story 3

"For you created my inmost being; you knit me together in my mother's womb, I praise you because I am fearfully and wonderfully made; Your works are wonderful, I know that full well."

Psalm 139:13-14

Psalm 139:13-14 states that God created my inmost being, He knit me together in my mother's womb, that I am fearfully and wonderfully made, and I "know that full well." Well, that was the problem. I didn't know that full well. I actually didn't like myself very much. There are two specific events that brought that to my attention.

The first was how I reacted to Mother's Day. Before my divorce, my husband at the time had made every Mother's Day miserable. It was not a very enjoyable day for me. Once divorced, I continued to be miserable on Mother's Day until one particular Mother's Day it hit me full force what I was doing. I was treating myself poorly. From that point on I began to plan my own Mother's Day and began to enjoy that day with my children. What is amazing is that now, as adults, they make every Mother's Day special!

The second issue that brought this to my attention was my feeling a failure as a parent. When my three children became teenagers I really didn't think I was doing well as a parent. I ended up going to a counselor who helped me to see that all parents have "issues" with their children and he helped me to better communicate with them. What came to the forefront, though, was the fact that I didn't like myself very well and that was affecting everything in my life.

The counselor suggested I find scripture to meditate on. It was Psalm 139: 13-14 that I chose because I did not "know it fully well." For a couple of weeks each morning I meditated on those two verses. I read and repeated it continually. It was surprisingly simple but what a difference it made. I still go back to meditate on this scripture from time to time because I go back to the old way of thinking from time to time.

Wendy

My Story 4

> *"But He was pierced for our transgressions, He was crushed for our iniquities; the punishment that brought us peace was upon Him, and by His wounds we are healed."*
>
> Isaiah 53:5

As she peered at me over her reading glasses while glancing down at my pathology report my doctor softly said, "What we are dealing with here is a small breast cancer." Those were the only words I can remember her saying to me on November 7, 2006, of which I can quote her word for word. Everything else from that point on is a blur. On my way back to my office I called and told my husband who immediately said "everything will be okay." But would it? I began praying and crying asking God to help me through this and to be able to deliver the message to my family and friends without scaring them to death. I was so worried that they would be worried. I think I was more upset about how they would take it than I was about the diagnosis. The first friend I told at work made the most profound statement of all, she said "Mary Alice, this is going to be real test of your faith" and immediately she knelt down and prayed with me. To this day those words still resonate in my soul. I am convinced that the reason for my trial was exactly that, a test for me to grow in the spirit and learn how to truly give God all of my burdens while trusting that He is capable of taking care of every little detail.

For 16 years I had thought the only way to raise a child was to worry about every little thing she did. I thought I had faith and was trusting God, after all I had been a Christian since I was 9 years old. I prayed continuously over concerns I had for her and others; however, I didn't think I was doing my part as a parent unless I was worrying as well. As it turns out not only did this test help me learn how to turn everything over to the Lord, it saved me from becoming alienated by my child.

When I got home that night, my husband and I told our daughter the news of my illness. They both were so strong. It was later on that night, when I overheard them in her room sobbing. I marched into the room and made a deal with them right then and there that if they would promise me that they would be alright, I would be alright as well. That became my motto for all of my family and friends. No giving in to the fear of the disease, only trusting God for a positive outcome.

As it turned out, I had a very aggressive type of cancer that had spread to my lymph nodes; therefore, treatment was going to entail 18 weeks of chemotherapy and 31 days of radiation after that. I had heard all of the horror stories about how sick the drugs could make me as well as what might be some other devastating side effects, but God was so merciful to me. I felt His presence with me in my weakest moments, even in the middle of the night when I couldn't sleep and it was just Him and me. I **knew** I was in His complete and total care and that I had to trust Him because there wasn't one thing in this world I could do to make this better. It was all up to Him! So, I trusted in Him.

I was never nauseous the first time, never had sores in my mouth (supposedly this type of chemo would cause that as well) and was convinced that I would not lose my hair. However, my doctor kept reassuring me that I would. And so it happened on New Year's Day, 2007. My husband noticed some loose hair on my pillow, and sure enough when I ran my fingers through it, there was plenty in my hand. So, I called my brother who uses clippers and has less hair than any of my other six siblings, and we went to work sitting in my garage clipping away until it was all gone. It was time to access the damage and as he hesitantly handed me the mirror, we both started dying laughing! I looked just like him!! We had never been told that we favored each other until then. But now, there was no denying it! It was a great moment.

After all of my treatments were over and I had been given a clean bill of health, I promised myself and God that I would share my story from fear to faith with anyone that would listen. I know now I really can do all things through Christ Jesus who strengthens me and so can you. Just don't let yourself have to get diagnosed with a serious illness to teach you how it's done.

May God bless each and every person that reads these words and know that ALL THINGS ARE POSSIBLE WITH GOD. DON'T EVER DOUBT THE POWER OF ALMIGHTY GOD!!!

Mary Alice

My Story 5

"Trust in the Lord with all thy heart, and lean not onto thy own understanding, in all thy ways acknowledge him, and He will direct thy path."
Proverbs 3: 5-6

"And we know that all things work together for good for those who love the Lord, for those who are called according to His purpose."
Romans 8:28

I have loved these scriptures for many years; however an experience that suddenly pierced my life has taught me more about the scriptures than I ever knew possible. Although I learned and continue to discover many lessons, I learned during this time that it is the scripture that works through us and not us that works through the scripture.

My life changed when I received a call and was told of my husband's 10 year infidelity. Simultaneously I was going through a difficult time with my church family. Personal attacks were common, so I lost the support of my brothers and sisters in Christ during this very grueling period. My trust of my husband was shattered and "if I was staying in this marriage" became my daily issue. I was truly alone, and darkness came over my life that lasted for many months.

Darkness can be difficult to say the least, but most of all, it is very lonely. Loneliness had been my constant companion, even from my childhood. In Christ I had discovered that though I may feel lonely, I was never alone, however the darkness caused me to question if God was truly there.

The number one question that I kept asking myself was, "Why?" I would hit my head with my hand and simultaneously ask "Why? Why? Why?" I would wake to the sound of wailing to only discover it was me. Grief enveloped me. I grieved the marriage I thought I had, and came to believe that sometimes death is easier. It was so very dark I had no hope and became so very angry with God I stopped reading His Words

I went through the motions of church, to include bible study, but I was frozen (lifeless). My prayers were more like yelling, and lacked any humility, only contained the honesty of how I was truly feeling.

In spite of the years that separate me from this time, writing these words returns me to that abyss, and tears well up in my eyes. I sought to find someone that understood. Everywhere I turned, including a counselor, there was no one who could say the words I longed to hear, "I understand."

My counselor let me know that in the book of Matthew the words of our Lord freed me from this marriage, and I could leave knowing that this would not be held against me by our Lord. However, He wanted me stay and try to heal the brokenness of my marriage. I felt that if people knew, they would only laugh at my choice. I became paranoid and felt as though everyone was looking at me for being so very stupid, and staying with a man that from all appearances did not love me. My fears had no foundation, because very few people knew what had happened.

What brought me out of the darkness? It was the scripture that never left me. When I questioned why, the Lord would remind me of Proverbs 3:5-6, that I must trust Him, not try and understand why this happened, and He would give me direction.

When I became angry, Romans 8:28 would emerge from Him, and the words, "All things" came to me, followed closely by "work together for good for those who love the Lord for those called according to His purpose." I knew I loved the Lord, and I began to want this event to be used for the good of my marriage, as well as to help someone else.

Ever so slowly, I began to see some light. Like Joseph in the pit, it was only in looking up I found my hope.

I have still not met another woman who has experienced what I have experienced, although I know that there are many out there. But, I have a Lord Jesus that knows far more about betrayal than I do. I love Him and often when I return to that place of unbearable pain, He says to me, "I understand, you are not alone", and I am reminded that He chose to allow Himself to be betrayed. His love is everlasting, and He is always with me. I was never alone.

Anonymous 2

My Story 6

"But you are a chosen people, a royal priesthood, a holy nation, a people belonging to God, that you may declare the praises of Him who called you out of the darkness into His wonderful light."

1 Peter 2:9

Why can't I believe that???? I have heard it all my life that I was chosen by God. Ok, if He knew what a mess I would turn out to be, WHY WOULD HE STILL CHOOSE ME?? Sometimes I feel like such a failure. Nothing is right. I don't smile right, I am not funny, I don't make people feel at ease, I can't keep the house clean or pretty, I don't make my kids or husband feel important enough. I can't do anything right.

I am afraid to tell all my wonderful Christian friends how I feel. I am afraid to tell even my non-Christian friends. I have this image that they all think and see me a certain way and if I ruined that, then what would I have?? They would also just 'pooh pooh' these feelings. "Oh you're so good, you're so lucky...blah blah blah". I do not feel any of these things.

I feel so alone. I struggle so hard to get up, smile and pretend all is well. I read scripture and see how God loves me, how He created me, and that He will never leave me. I believe all that, but …yet there is still the 'but'.

If HE loves me so much, why do I dislike myself so much? I have heard folks say that by thinking bad of myself I am telling God I know more than He does. That thought helps for a while. If God made me and He likes me, then I should not argue with the Boss, right?

I heard a preacher say once that God sees me as Glorious! Me glorious? That's a pretty good thought. It's hard to believe. But again, who am I to argue with the Boss?

How about this one: 'God sees me through Jesus filled lenses". That's one to think about. When God puts on glasses to look at me, He sees Jesus first. Kind of like the camera filters they use to make people look younger! I am filtered by Christ!!!

Then there is the good ole: God doesn't make junk or God's not finished with me yet, and I am a child of the King! Remember in the fairytales, the king always has a special place for his princess!

I still feel like a failure, but after just writing these down, I feel a peace about my failures. I can smile and think "yep, I am a mess, a screw up, and sometimes maybe even a little useless' but if I remind myself what God feels about me, I feel better!

Who cannot smile at knowing that you are glorious, seen through Jesus filters, and are the princess of the King? Even when I screw up, the King loves His daughter… me! The King always gives His little girl another chance. The King of Kings gives me grace.

God understands my depression, my struggles and my difficulties. I may disappoint my family, my work, and myself, but I can't disappoint my Lord. Because He loves me. He has to, why would anyone make junk???

Claire

My Story 7

> *"For I know the plans I have for you"* declares the Lord *"plans to prosper you and not to harm you, plans to give you a hope and a future. Then you will call on me and come and pray to me and I will listen to you."*
>
> Jeremiah 29:11-12

Now I had a problem with verse eleven of Jeremiah 29. God promises His plans are to prosper us. Not harm us. But what I was going through and what I was feeling felt like harm to me.

I had been told I had precancerous cells in my uterus. All I could hear was the cancer part. Never mind that the doctor said precancerous, not cancer. I had seen enough family members deal with cancer to know this was going to be tough.

I'll admit I was terrified. I called my husband crying and I told him what the doctor said. He told me not to worry we would get through this. Not to worry? Was he crazy? How could I not worry? I didn't think I could get through any of this. I didn't think I was strong enough to handle it.

You know what? I'm not strong enough. Not by myself. With God's help, family support and friends at church who came around me and showed me that God didn't leave me. He didn't forsake me. He wasn't punishing me for some wrong in my life. With my family and friends supporting me I learned God's love was very deep and wide. I learned more about grace, trust, and true worship during this time of crisis. I also found a deeper connection with God.

He promises if we seek Him, we will find Him. He also promises to listen. He even listened when I was crying, begging for healing or yelling at Him in anger. Yes, I was very angry. Angry because my dream of becoming a mommy someday seemed to be slipping from my grasp.

Then I heard a new song at church. It struck me right in the middle of my fear, anger and grief. The words say "weak made strong in the Savior's love. Through the storm He is Lord, Lord of all". I realized that no matter what He is Lord of all, even the storms of life. And if he was closing one door, some day He would open another.

I thought God took too long in healing me, but His timing is perfect. As I learned to let go of the anger, fear and grief, and learned to trust that is when my healing began. Both physically and spiritually, I prospered in renewed faith, deeper friendships, and a love and peace that truly does surpass all understanding.

Kathryn

My Story 8

"...being confident of this, that He who began a good work in you will carry it onto completion until the day of Christ Jesus."

Philippians 1:6

I grew up Jewish until I was 8 and then Greek Orthodox until I was 17.

I really did not have a relationship with God. I thought he was some authoritative figure that was harsh, judgmental, and unforgiving.

July 5, 1990 is when a doctor found blockages in my neck it, was my first office visit with her and from there my journey started. I was diagnosed with Takayasu's Disease. It is a very rare vascular disease that is usually found in an autopsy after you stroke out. One of the nurses treating me invited me to a nondenominational church. I walked in thinking I was dreaming, the people were standing up clapping and singing it was nothing I had ever experienced before. I was in treatment for 2.5 years doing 3 rounds of chemotherapy and steroids. I decided I couldn't do this in my own strength, so I reached out to God because I had learned that he was a kind and loving God who had forgiven me of the things I had done. His Love and

Grace are given freely. His Love is unconditional. I eventually went into remission.

I was married to an emotionally abusive husband and there were many times I wanted to leave him but I made a promise to God for better or worse. Little did I know that the worse was coming. I believe that God is the pilot of our lives and we are the passengers. We just don't know how much turbulence or how many layovers we will have until we reach our final destination.

When we came back from North Carolina Frank was diagnosed with bladder cancer. Part of it was because of a choice he made, which was to smoke. His suffering was extreme and I don't know why he had to endure that, but I will tell you neither of us questioned God. In fact our faith is what kept us strong. All of our lives are temporal, some shorter than others. For example, my nephew died 6 months later at the age of 30. God continued to supply all of my needs. I was only making $13.00 an hour with my rent at $1895.00 per month. I had my mother and daughter at home. My landlord told me to pay what I could and The Nevada Cancer Institute paid for my rent, gas and food for 5 months. I ended up working for my landlord and he is still a dear friend who has helped me immensely. My meeting him was definitely a divine appointment.

So I am doing life and last Jan 2012 I am diagnosed with Hypertrophic Obstructive Cardiomyopathy. It is another rare genetic disease. It is called Sudden Death Syndrome (Athletes drop dead from it) but I never said "Why Me God" I said "God, thank you that it was detected". Last year was full of doctor appointments and challenges with medicine, but I Never lost faith. I just said "another bump in the road". During all of this,

I received the settlement for my husband's death which I had fought for 7 long years. It is what is giving me the opportunity to buy my house.

I did have a scare in October at The Mayo Clinic they were testing me for Fabry's Disease and the initial test came back positive. I would have had to have an infusion treatment once a week for the rest of my life. But I had many people praying for me and the second test came back negative. But yet again, I never got mad at God, because I felt it is just another bump in the road, not a stop sign. There are so many more people that are sicker than. I still have challenges with my heart and the medicine is still not right. But I have never lost hope and still cling to God's promises.

I have been showered with multitudes of blessings. I have wonderful friends and two beautiful daughters. I have a beautiful home and a wonderful church family.

So why am I telling you all this? I am telling you, so you know even in your darkest hour, no matter what we have done; God is there with his unconditional love. It is called Grace. He is there to give you the strength to get thru anything. All you have to do is ask and believe. We are given free will to do good or bad, and that is why the world has evil. Not because of God.

I believe with every fiber of my bones, that every person we meet is a Divine Appointment. With God there are no accidents. I just know that I have a Joy in my heart that is only there because of my relationship with God and I want that for you.

Dee

My Story 9

"...and call upon Me in the day of trouble; I will deliver you, and you will honor Me."

Psalm 50:15

Years ago when our youngest son was in middle school, he spent one summer on his bed, watching MTV and talking on the phone with his girlfriend. The young lady and her family had just moved away. When the first month phone bill arrived, it was over $500. After a long discussion about family phone rules, I figured all was well, until the next month's bill came. Now we owed over $1000. This was not an amount I could simply write a check for and be done with. The amount owed to the phone company was a huge burden on my husband and me as making ends meet was already a difficult task. I took on a second job to pay off the bill. (And had the phone cut off.)

I don't have to tell any mother or wife just how stressful working two jobs are. With trying to fit in laundry, grocery shopping, cooking and cleaning, I was tired and always running behind.

The convenience store was a family-run bait and tackle store. Here you could get a fishing license, buy gas or pick up coffee or a Pepsi. I worked Saturdays and Sundays in addition to my full time weekly job. On Sunday mornings, usually just 2 of us worked. The Grandmother ran the front and registers while I would fill up the drink coolers and clean the minnow tanks.

Even though I regretted not being able to worship on Sunday mornings, I felt confident that the good Lord understood. But one particular Sunday morning, things were not going to be normal. Two unknown men shook my world.

This particular Sunday morning, a family member came by with breakfast biscuits for us. I ate my biscuit and as the other two chatted, I thought it would be a perfect time to go into the walk-in cooler to get chilled drinks to start restocking the individual coolers. As I came out of the walk-in with a basket full of drink bottles, the door slammed shut loudly behind me. I came up the main aisle and saw a figure at the front door that was shouting loudly, "who else is here?" I am answering, "no one else" as all the while this guy is waving a sawed off shotgun and telling me to get over there and on the ground. Nothing is really making any sense at this time. The figure is dressed all in black. There is something resembling a fencing mask over his face. Tube socks are covering his hands and arms. Looking in the direction he is pointing for me to go, I see another similar figure and finally realize what is happening. We are being robbed.

Two of us were forced to lie on the ground with the sawed off shotgun pointed at our heads while Grandma was directed to hand over last night's receipts. The men order us to take off our jewelry and hand over our purses. We all complied. As I returned to the face down position on the floor, I realized today may be the end of my life here on earth. My life didn't flash before me. Instead, all I could think about was I never got to tell my family goodbye and I love them. I let everyone sleep in as I left for work that morning.

The other family member who had stopped by with breakfast was starting to panic beside me on the floor. I thought;" she needs to calm down or we will all be killed". I took her hand and gently whispered to look down, not up. I quietly started to say the Lord's Prayer, hoping to calm her nerves and mine. The phone had started ringing, and ringing. One of the gunmen yanked it from the box and threw it across the store. The person calling was another employee and knew it was odd that no one would answer. She headed to the store right away. Everything was over in just a few minutes, and yet it seemed like a lifetime.

After the men realized they were not going to get much, we all were ordered into the walk-in cooler where they locked us inside. Then they left. We crawled through the front of the walk-in and then called the police. Next, I called my husband, my hero who was there in just a few minutes to comfort me.

It turned out the two men were a father and his son who were hooked on drugs. The duo had also robbed a couple of banks and two or three other convenience stores. Police found our jewelry and purses in the attic of the father's home. They are both serving life sentences in Federal prison on bank robbery convictions.

There were some issues left to deal with. We all had to get new driver's license and cancel our checking accounts. There were police forms to fill out and questions to answer. I personally could not sleep or eat. I had bloody nightmares. It became so bad, I was losing weight and soon my husband made me report what I ate each day. My coworkers encouraged me to eat by offering snacks. Sometimes all I could manage to get down was a plain piece of bread or a few saltine crackers I ended up with posttraumatic stress syndrome. But with my faith in God, I overcame.

The story really does have a happy ending. Our son grew to be a fine and upstanding man of whom we are very proud. The phone bill somehow got paid off. My husband once again was there when I needed him most and to this day he is still my hero.

> *"For I know the plans I have for you,"* declares the LORD. *"Plans to prosper you and not to harm you, plans to give you hope and a future."*
> Jeremiah 29:11

This passage gave me peace and comfort to know it was not His plan I die that day. I had a promise of a future. My faith helped heal me. Slowly my life returned and once again, I could hear the birds sing each morning. You also have been promised through His grace and blessing. Amen.

Barbara

My Story 10

"Oh Lord, You have searched me and You know me…"
Psalm 139

Bitter or Better?

As a young woman growing up in Fayetteville North Carolina, I remember a sermon that our preacher gave that made a profound impression on me. The pastor spoke about how circumstances in one's life can either make us bitter or better. This really struck a chord with me because at the age of five I had been diagnosed with rheumatoid arthritis.

Living with a debilitating disease was and still is very frustrating and at times embarrassing. There are times when I am too stiff to get myself dressed or wash my own hair. When doing simple things around the house will take all the energy I have, and then some.

Sometimes I may want to ask God why me? However, I have learned there is a bigger lesson here, through God's grace I have learned that it is not about me, but it is about Him. Just simply resting and trusting totally in Him is what I have and am still learning! His strength is made perfect in my weakness.

Learning to show GOD's glory is what all of us should strive to do regardless of our circumstances.

All of us struggle with hardships in some form or another. All of us are fighting our own private battles whether it's physical illness, financial loss or relationship failures. Nevertheless, as I have been blessed to live the life that He has given me, I realize just how special every one of us is. He has an extraordinary job for each of us to do if we will open ourselves up to HIS healing and trust in HIM. GOD can take every facet of our lives and make something meaningful out of it, HE can make us better.

My favorite scripture is Psalm 139 because it speaks of how GOD knew us before we were born. No matter how far away we get from Him, HE is faithful, and HE is there. No matter our circumstances, GOD has a plan and can use our brokenness and our inability to bless and encourage others. GOD made only one you, and He has a job that only you can do. Regardless of what you have been through or what you are going through; the good, bad or ugly, GOD wants us to be better and make this a better place for each other.

For my own personal testimony, I have learned that being confined to a wheelchair does not define me as a person but of being a child of GOD. There is no higher calling than that. My challenge to you is that no matter what failures, heartaches, or disappointments you have in life, give them to Christ and let Him use them for good. You never know how your life and the lives of those around you will be changed for the better.

Stella

My Story 11

"But He said to me, "My grace is sufficient for you, for my power is made perfect in weakness." Therefore I will boast all the more gladly about my weaknesses, so that Christ's power may rest on me."
2 Corinthians 12:9

"And we know that in all things God works for the good of those who love and him, who have been called according to his purpose."
Romans 8:28

Just because I'm a Christian doesn't mean my struggles will automatically disappear. Condemnation and convictions are two sides of one coin. Revealing something in our lives could involve one or both. Condemnation comes only from Satan. Condemnation is passing judgment upon someone. Conviction has a proof of guilt. Recently I experienced both but with very different results.

In the past I had struggled with sexual desires and sins. I thought that struggle was gone until someone re-entered my life. The battle in my head and heart began again. In my own strength, I began to try to fight it, which was not a smart thing to do. In my mind I began losing the battle as my thoughts became focused solely on another human being. I kept telling myself that I was asking God what to do so that was okay. Yes, He wants us to ask Him what to do but He wants to do it through us, not have us do it in our own strength. We never have that much power alone and on our own. God removed those people in my life, to remove the false God and remove the temptation. I was very hurt and angry at first, but when I look at things through His eyes and not my own, I see the plan is for me never to meet any need I have physical or emotional through another human because they can never fulfill it.

The condemnation brought shame, hurt, anger, and fear from others and of God. The conviction brought hurt and sadness but it also brought revelation and brought me closer to God. The condemnation will always attack the identity I have been given in Christ and try to convince me that I am worthless, unloved, and not accepted. The conviction will never attack the identity I have in Christ, but will always discipline and correct the action that I have done which was against Gods will for me. Through both I usually learn a lesson. Sometimes that lesson brings loss and pain. Just because my life continues to involve pain and sadness, doesn't mean my identity in Christ changes and it doesn't mean God has left me or isn't real. He loves me. He accepts me. I am His child. No choice or mistake I make can change that.

Amy

My Story 12

> *"So do not fear, for I am with you. Do not be dismayed, for I am your God. I will strengthen you and help you; I will uphold you with my righteous right hand."*
>
> Isaiah 41:10

Domestic violence victim. Abused. Battered wife. I heard all these labels all my life, but never thought that those words would one day describe me. But the man was supposedly the love of my life; my parents even said that they had never seen a more perfect match. Little did we all know what was going to happen in the little blue house on the corner for the next 6 months.

Yes it was only 6 months, it doesn't sound like much time. I tell myself that too, somehow trying to make it less than what it really was. But those 6 months were the darkest, scariest, and loneliest 6 months of my entire young life. My ex would go through cycles of how to abuse me every day, but he perfected every way of doing so; physically, verbally, mentally, emotionally, and sexually. Honestly, I would love to go into every little detail of the abuse and turn it into a hate-fest. But unfortunately, that would probably hinder the whole forgiveness process.

The memories and pain can haunt me daily sometimes, even years later. But with the painful memories comes another strong memory. Even more then the fear and pain that I remember feeling, I remember the overwhelming presence of and peace from God. Don't get me wrong, I was hurt, angry, and confused with/at/by God. But in those times of darkness, I was all alone except that He was with me. And I know that, because without Him I wouldn't be here today. I grew up memorizing Isaiah 41:10, it was my favorite verse: "So do not fear, for I am with you. Do not be dismayed, for I am your God. I will strengthen you and help you; I will uphold you with my righteous right hand". I know that without God's help, I would not be here today. He gave me the strength to leave before I was killed. In the greatest times of fear, I felt Him with me in a way that I have never felt before or since. In a way I sort of miss that.

With the help of God, family, and friends I was able to escape and rebuild my life. So just know that in the darkest, scariest, and loneliest times of life it can feel like all is lost. But I encourage you, from one survivor to another; don't fear, because He is with you. Don't be dismayed, because He is your God. He will strengthen you and help you. He will uphold you with His righteous right hand.

De Anne

My Story 13

"Come to me, all you who are weary and burdened, and I will give you rest. Take my yoke upon you and learn from me, for I am gentle and humble in heart, and you will find rest for your souls. For My yoke is easy and my burden is light."
Matthew 11:28-30

I could tell by the doctor's face that the news was bad. I was alone with baby#2, who was quietly playing in her hospital bed, paper cup taped to her little head to keep the IV line in her skull. The doctor said the staff in the genetics office cried when the results came in. My unborn child would also be born with Cystic Fibrosis (CF). I was to be the mother of three little girls, all with CF, and all with a prognosis of life in hospitals, medicines, and early death. All of my babies!

I was alone, scared, and my heart hurt.

I did not ask God the 'why' question at that point. Yet I did ask Him the "How" questions: How am I going to raise these precious little girls to live life to the fullest when it will be full of pills, treatments and IVs? How do I live everyday knowing that my babies may die before age 15? How can I do this and not go crazy with the fear of the future? How can

I survive the pain to my heart with every cough or cry from my babies?

God answered all my "How am I..?" questions with "Let Me". He answered my cry and gave me peace. My babies actually belonged to God. He lent these little girls to me. God had entrusted their lives, as difficult as it may be to me, and He will not let me do this alone.

The Lord has kept His promise all these years. I have felt the comforting arm of Jesus around my shoulders when I have been crying uncontrollably alone in the car, calling to Him in pain. I have felt His peace when my little girl was being rushed to the ICU while I was pumping the O2 bag into her lungs, watching her turn blue. He gave me strength when driving the two hours from the hospital to work, check on the other girls and then drive back to the hospital so I could spend the night with the hospitalized daughter. He gave me endurance when I would have to get up two times a night to administer home IVs for three weeks so I could still function at work and home.

As I watch the CF take parts of my daughters' lives away, I cry silent and hidden tears. I dread the day if this disease wins. I do not know how I will survive, but He has been with me and I know He will not desert me. He will uphold me; He will give me strength, for He is my God!!

Andrea

My Story 14

"...who forgives all your sins and heals all your diseases, who redeems your life with love and compassion."
                                                    Psalm 103:3-4

But for the grace of God…

The relationship that I have with God today is so different from what it was when I was growing up. Actually, I didn't really have a relationship with Him as a child. I believed in God but I feared Him. My perception of God was distorted and caused me a lot of anguish. I saw God as this huge, heavenly authority that was sitting up there just waiting for me to screw up. I lived with this anxiety that God was going to get me and once He did it wasn't going to be good.

Every time I did something I knew God would not approve of, I cringed. I literally lived my life ducking and trying to avoid or hide from God! I viewed Him as a punishing God, an angry God and felt that He couldn't possibly love me and I definitely didn't feel He would help me in any way. I always felt that God was out to get me.

I wasn't a bad person; I was a sick person in need of healing. I made many bad choices in my young life and suffered many consequences for them. I knew right from wrong, I had a desire to be a good person but I lacked spiritual guidance. In my early adult life I only turned to God when I was backed into a corner by life's circumstances. The only prayer I knew was, "Oh God, please help me! If you get me out of this one, I promise I'll never do this again!" I didn't pray to God, I bargained with Him. When I did get out of whatever trouble I found myself in, I quickly forgot my promise to God, giving myself the credit for managing to slide out of some situation and went about my merry way. Of course my way was anything but merry, in actuality it was miserable! Life was hard and there seemed to be one crisis after another! The fact that I was creating much of my own hardships seemed to elude me. I had fallen victim to the blame game! Did you catch the word I used? Victim... I became a victim of my own life. A victim of circumstances, or so I thought. The pain of living became greater and greater as time went on. The truth was I wasn't a victim, I was an addict. I suffered from the disease of addiction and my denial of the truth nearly killed me.

There's an old saying; 'when the pain gets great enough, we get willing'. This proved true for me. I had a very high tolerance for pain!!! It took a lot before I hit bottom! There were a couple of times that I thought I was at my bottom, but I had only scraped it and bounced off it a time or two, ready to try it my way again and again and again and again... I was a living example of the definition of insanity. I continued to do the same thing over and over again, always thinking it was going to be different this time! Oh it was different alright, it kept getting worse each time I denied help or thought I could handle things on my own! At the tender age of 22 I was defeated. I was physically sick, mentally and emotionally drained, and spiritually empty. Although I was still breathing, I was no longer living; I just existed like the living dead. The word joy was not in my vocabulary, happy was a joke and life had nothing to offer. Here I was, a single mom with 2 young boys and I was already wore out, used up and done in. I had gone to see a doctor, convinced I was dying. I had referred myself because I was sure I had cancer and that's what was wrong with me. Of course this doctor assured me if I was indeed dying, it wasn't from cancer and I think he may have suggested I might need to look at my lifestyle. I wasn't happy with his diagnosis or lack of diagnosis and I dismissed his suggestions I needed to look at how I was living. I think back to that today and it still amazes me that I would rather have cancer than admit I was an addict. I later read what he wrote in his evaluation of me to my primary care physician. He referred to me as 'morbid', stating that he had never seen a young woman in such a morbid state. He was not the first person to use the word morbid in a description of me; in fact there were two other occasions where this term was used to describe me towards the end of my active addiction. I was a sick young girl, I suffered from the disease of addiction and I was powerless to do anything about it.

How did I get that way? You name it, drugs, alcohol, men, deep buried hurts, fast lifestyle...but most of all I wound up where I was as a result of running just as fast I could from God. I never believed I was good enough for God and although I believed in God, I didn't believe He was interested in doing anything for me. I am so thankful that He showed me how very wrong I was.

My will was so strong, so rebellious; I was so full of me, myself and I! My pride and ego nearly killed me. I was living in a two room apartment with my kids in NJ when I hit bottom. What I remember most about that is I had an entire bee hive in the ceiling of the bedroom filled with carpenter bees. I realized they were there when both my children were stung after I had put them to bed. After that we all stayed in the living room on two couches. While my boys slept I kept vigil at the bedroom door sitting up at night with a can of bug spray and a fly swatter. As the bees crawled out from under the door, I would spray and swat at them to kill them. As if things weren't crazy enough, I was allergic to bees! I told the apartment superintendent about them and his response to me was, "When you leave, I'll get rid of the bees!" I was behind in my rent, the cable had been shut off, the phone was getting ready to be disconnected and I was behind on my electric bill. On top of that I had roaches that were made of steel! One night I had a roast with potatoes and carrots in the oven on 200 degrees just to keep it warm, but that didn't keep the roaches out of there! I look back at this time in my life and it feels like some kind of a bad dream. It was definitely a nightmare!

As if this was not bad enough, the final days before my life changed were the days I can never forget. The kids and I had gone to stay with a friend for a couple of days so I could figure out what I was going to do. I'd been here before, many times I made plans to change my life but I always failed to follow through with them. My stay with this friend evolved into a series of events that would finally lead me to hit what I pray is my last bottom. To summarize the end of my active addiction, I often say I was probably 10 minutes from losing my kids and 15 minutes from going to prison. Instead, but for the grace of God I found the rooms of recovery. I like to say that God led me to the rooms and the rooms led me to God. I had planned to move to Oregon, but God clearly had a different plan. My mother came to get us in NJ and drove us to NC, where she and my brothers now live and I would call home as well. God gave me another chance at life.

I did change my lifestyle. I gave up the drugs and alcohol. My mind started to clear and I started to grow up again! I began my journey with God and was delighted to learn that He was not the angry, punishing God I once thought. He is a loving and caring God! His mercy is unending and His grace is amazing! God saved me. He watched and waited patiently until I crashed and He gently picked me up and began to put me back together again. He showed me He loved me and I was worth saving. I am His child. He never gave up on me. I had given up on Him…

October 4, 1983 is the day I began my spiritual journey and my relationship with the Lord. Since that day I haven't taken a drink or gotten high, and God has been my constant companion as well as my source of strength. No matter what happens in my life today, I trust He will always provide whatever I need when I need it. There have been times when I felt far from Him, when I had fallen into an attitude of indifference or complacency, but I now know that God is always right there, whenever the pain gets great enough and I'm ready to let go and let God! I've made many mistakes since beginning my journey with God but my God is a God of second chances, and third chances and fourth chances.....He's faithful and His love is unconditional. He is a good God! I am very thankful to know this, not just in my head but in my heart. If He was not a God of many chances then there'd be no hope for many of us! Human beings are flawed, we are broken, all of us and we all need a Savior. Thanks to His son Jesus, He has provided a way for us to be saved from our sins or as I like to say, from our own skin. His blood covers us with forgiveness. Today I try to live the best I can and to be willing to be teachable, to grow in God's will, to serve Him through serving others and to cultivate an attitude of gratitude in the journey. It's in this way I glorify God and thank Him for all He has done for me, through me and in me.

Through my experience I've learned as we grow and honestly mature in our faith through Christ we desire to live as He tells us to live. We're more willing to live with obedience and seek God's guidance. However, we will always fall short and for those times that we fall into sin, we can have confidence that God allows us to return to Him with welcoming arms, lovingly guiding us back to the place where we belong, walking with the ultimate authority, a loving God who will never leave us or forsake us. The spiritual journey is about progress not perfection. I will never be perfect but I strive to live as Christ lived. That is a lifelong process. Knowing that He is a loving and caring God helps me to want to do better and to try again. Giving up is not an option because God never gives up on me, I don't ever want to give up on Him again!

Thank you God for all of the chances you've given me. I will *'bee'* forever grateful! Some of us need a little extra motivation and God finds a way to provide this. He truly works in mysterious ways. I believe or rather I *'bee*-lieve' He was trying to motivate me to make a change! I can take a hint!

But for the grace of God I can live peacefully, love freely & forgive faithfully today…and live clean so I can reach out to other addicts seeking recovery and a new way to live, freely giving to them what was so freely given to me. Grateful for God's grace, His mercy and His unconditional love that guides my life.

Lynda

My Story 15

"For God has not given us a spirit of fear and timidity, but of power, love, and self-discipline."
                                             2 Timothy 1:7

"A Window"

Can I look through a window of your world?
Can I see the love you've known?
I only want to touch that smile
And feel the happiness inside
I want to walk behind you
And place my feet within the footprints of your life
Can I look through a window of your world?
Can I know the joy that you've known?
I want to run and play
I want to fall and cry
I want to be surrounded by those arms of love
Can I look through a window of your world?
Can I feel the understanding that you've known
I want to touch the warm beating heart
As it gives life to your eyes
I want to grasp the crayon, which gives color to your world
I want to experience that freedom of security
Can I look through a window of your world?"

In the past I was ruled by generational sins and choices of a family stuck within tradition and the walls of confinement. For many years, obedience has been confused with gaining respect. Control has been confused with helping. Punishment has been confused with discipline and grace. I began to look in the windows of other's lives to find the things I wanted and needed. My life to me seemed normal but, at the same time I didn't like it and wanted something else.

All of my life I have been paralyzed by fear, the fear of physical abuse, mental abuse, sexual abuse and abandonment. Around every corner was someone wanting something, needing something. I had been repeatedly raped, molested, abused and threatened by many people in my life and thought this was life for everyone. I felt nowhere was safe anymore. It happened in a church, outside a church, in the home and outside the home. Friends, family, and acquaintances were all involved. I didn't know whom to trust anymore. All things had strings attached… gifts, love, it didn't matter what it was. It came with a string.

At an early age I learned that things had strings attached and I had to wear a mask to accommodate them all. I was told to never speak unless spoken to, so I also learned quickly to express anything real about me in hidden messages of art and writing. I began drawing and painting at an early age. I would hide in an old oak tree after school to draw, read, or write whatever I could. My hiding became an internal and external way of life for me. I could find a way of life I liked inside my books and inside the stories I would write or draw out in my art.

When you are abused life seems to stop in some ways. You don't know how to go beyond the point something important to life is taken from you. Those around you become enemies no matter who they may be, simply because they may carry a characteristic of the abuser. The environment around you also becomes something you tend to question because you look at it from the prospective of whether you can be hurt there or not. The past is never allowed to be left behind. It wants to never lay its head down, never wants to slow down to be worked through so that it can be understood, and become in anyway intimate with the present world.

When I was away from my family I tried to break free of the bars surrounding me through the activities I chose. I hungered and thirsted for more energy, excitement, and peace and would do anything to be outside where there were no walls. But I continued to walk in the same worn out path given to me. I refused to take inner leaps that would allow for new permanent chances and changes. I couldn't make myself talk about things I felt and things I had experienced. I wanted someone to blame and instead drove myself deeper into insanity. Even though I wanted to go forward, my body and mind had stopped in the past and didn't want to allow me to catch up because this meant in some way I would need to begin a path I didn't know or understand. My life was complete contradictions.

I constantly looked for "love" in other people's actions and facial expressions. I wanted some visual to place with that word, Love. I never got the same one twice. I was told "I love ya", by friends. I was told "I love you" by those who called themselves friends or even family but instead only wanted to touch me in some way or take something from me. It isn't just a pattern I see now though, it is a perception and a way of living in a lot of ways.

My river of peace came from a bottle that always had an end. It constantly needed to start over so it never allowed me a place to lay my head.

Today I see myself struggling with determination to find a way out of the prison of the past. The doors are open, the chains are off, but I feel trapped somewhere between the past and a future I want to be. I repeatedly hear "The scene of the crime is the mind". Sometimes I continue to be ruled by the walls built by tradition and confinement within the thoughts of my mind.

I am loved just as the Father Loves Jesus. That's hard to write even today but no less true. I'm learning that I view God through a filter just like a lens filter that is dirty because of its environment. The only way to change that filter is to allow God to transform my mind. God the Father is teaching me the moment by moment process of sanctification that is rooted in a free gift with NO strings attached. He loved me before I was even born to the maximum amount possible.

Amie

My Story 16

"Blessed is the man who perseveres under trial, because when he has stood the test, he will receive the crown of life that God has promised to those who love him"

James 1:12

If you had met me seven years ago, you would get one of two impressions: annoying overachiever goody two shoes or a girl with a lot of determination.

To say I was determined would almost be an understatement. At the end of my junior year in high school I was in a fight with my Dad over why he wouldn't let me run for school president for my senior year. The fact that I was president of a few clubs already, taking eight AP classes and working after school didn't faze this stubborn headed teenage know-it-all. It seemed like the world would be mine, just like I had always been told.

However, if I compare where I was then to who I am today, I find one word describes me best: *failure*. Just one year into my college career, my parents and doctors decided I needed to stop going to school. You see, I have Cystic Fibrosis (CF), and from 2005 through 2010, I was hospitalized every six months or so. I would cough up blood for no apparent reason. I needed to get a port-a catheter at the end of my freshman year in college, and despite the fact that I had been living this life of in and out of the hospital every few months for 19 years, I believe the port was the final straw for my parents. To this day they would tell you that I was working myself into the grave. But that's not how I saw it. I was accomplishing dreams, hoping to change kid's lives with my work post-graduation, I was proving CF wrong. The damage that stopping me did emotionally and mentally, may never fully heal – I still look back in anguish, disappointment, and even anger.

Growing up I kept James 1:12 close to my heart, "Blessed is the man who remains steadfast under trial, for when he has stood the test he will receive the crown of life, which God has promised to those who love him." (ESV) Mostly thinking that no matter how bad life would get that God somehow would see that despite it all I was trying to honor Him with my life and He would reward me for it. But being knocked off my determined stride took an unprecedented amount out of me, so much so that here I am 6 years later still unable to fully move forward.

Yes, God has done a lot with my life since having to quit school, but I find myself still sitting here fighting off the feelings of Job's wife, wanting to throw everything He took away from me in front of His face, and begin to deny Him on little levels. Sometimes I remind myself how much Sarah, Hannah, and Elizabeth all waited on God and that while my life hasn't gone as planned I need to stay strong in Him and wait for His timing. It's so much easier said than done though.

Sometimes I wish that those cliché Christian sayings were true, you know the ones that promise everything will be great, because in the end it will be. In the here and now, though, it never feels joyous. Years later it still feels almost as painful as when it first began. To say that my faith hasn't taken a hit by this would be a lie. My faith is challenged daily, hourly, and sometimes even every minute — to be like Job, or his wife. Some days it's an easy turn back towards the One who has a much bigger plan then my little hissy fit over being forced out of school, and some days it's all I can do to even remember that I need to talk to Him or even thank Him for something.

Am I a failure in any stretch of the word? No! Unfortunately there are days when that word gets the best of me. Knowing though, that my God is still using me, loving me, and allowing me to glorify Him in ways I had never imagined because I limited myself with my plans, is quite an amazing feat. Proverbs 19:21 (NLT) "You can make many plans, but the LORD's purpose will prevail." If I allow myself to be molded into the plans that He has for me, instead of holding on to this idealized "failed" past, that may be the most fulfilling life after all. I just have to step out of the way.

Rebeka

My Story 17

"I have written these things to you who believe in the name of the Son of God, so that you will have eternal life."

1 John 5:13

When I was a child I went to church pretty regular. I mean, once we settled in a place where Daddy would find a job, we'd get registered for school and then Momma would find a church for us to go to. It was all pretty standard, as far as I figured. We'd moved a lot up and down the east coast by the time I was in the fourth grade. When we finally settled down to stay, it was in my father's hometown in North Carolina.

Momma would try to get in some Bible reading with us most nights before bed. When we got a little older and could read for ourselves, we would sit around the kitchen table and take turns reading the scriptures she'd chosen for us that day.

My father was what I guess you would call today a "binge" alcoholic. He'd go for weeks, sometimes months without a drink and then one Friday evening he'd show up drunk, taking all of his frustrations out on us kids and Momma. He'd go get his shotgun or rifle or sometimes a knife and "hold us hostage" so to speak until something would change his mind and he'd get up and walk away or leave the house all together.

When I look back on those moments in my life, they seem almost surreal. Like, could that have really happened? But I know they did. It happened over and over again in my childhood.

I remember going to bed and crying myself to sleep praying that God would please let my Daddy die before he was able to come back home. Then in the morning he'd be in the bedroom asleep and would not say a thing to any of us for days. I can remember my brother and me begging my mother to leave him and go to our Grandma's house in Alabama, but she acted as if she didn't hear us. So we just came to accept that this was our lot in life. And it was, until the week of spring revival in 1975 at a little country church in that same town.

The preacher had been preaching on Heaven most of the week and what you had to do to do to go there. Well, I was really trying hard to figure out "what it was" that I had to do because it still wasn't clear to me. And I knew I wanted to go to heaven! In my 12 year old mind and heart, all I could think of was that I did not want to go to the other place he also talked about that week. So on the way to the church on a Friday night, the last day of revival, I asked my Momma what was it he said we had to do to go to Heaven. All she could tell me was to walk up the aisle and talk to the preacher. So that's what I did. But as I remember it, I floated up that aisle. I can't tell you how I got to the preacher, but I did. I told him what I wanted and he knelt down with me and led me in the sinner's prayer.

There was no doubt that the Holy Spirit came to dwell within me that night at that moment. I knew when I prayed, I had made a decision that would change me forever. I guess I also thought that if Daddy ended up killing us one of those awful nights when he would come home drunk, that I would go to be with God when it happened.

I went to school the following Monday sharing the Good News that I was saved and born again and that I was going to Heaven when I died. And do you know that most of the kids in my 6th grade classroom had no idea what I was talking about? I remember it making me sad and realizing that I had to tell others about what had happened to me. Because of my salvation through Jesus' blood I was able to eventually forgive my father and my mother as well, for keeping us in the home with him. I was able to stop praying for death to come to him and prayed that he would see the light of Jesus. I spent time reading the scriptures every day in a new way because now the Spirit was living in me and helping me to understand what I hadn't before. I could pray now knowing that as I asked for forgiveness of my sins God would hear my prayers and give me comfort that I could not understand.

I wish I could tell you that my father came to his senses and to the Lord and changed miraculously over night, but he didn't. It took years for him to finally get to that point, but I *can* tell you this: when the Holy Spirit came into my life, He changed me in a way that I knew I was God's child. NO more wondering if there was a God and if He cared, or if He knew what was going on in my life. I came to know that God sees it all and He allows a certain amount in our lives for various reasons that for the most part, only He knows why. I also have learned that everyone comes to Him in the way that is personal to them. We each have a story to tell. Life gets dirty and even as followers of Christ, we make bad choices and there are consequences for those choices. I learned that my father grew up in a home where he wasn't shown much love at all and didn't know how to show it to others. Through God's Word, the Holy Spirit and His people, God has shown me how I need to work on *me* daily to be the Jesus that others can see. Because it may be the only "Jesus" they'll ever see.

Mary Beth

MyStory 18

"Cast all your anxiety on Him because He cares for you."

1 Peter 5:7

I work on the fifth floor but we also have offices on the fourth floor of our office building. There are occasions when I have a need to conduct business on the other floors. The office building is an older building but in a very nice part of the town.

Usually I take the elevator, even though it is only one floor down. Now first of all you must understand I have an elevator phobia. They scare me to death. I hate the creaking noises and vibrations they make while moving. I can get dizzy and nauseous. I am certain that when I die, it will be in an elevator.

This day, I was on four going back up to the fifth. I got in the elevator and pushed 5. Nothing happened. Dead silence. No funny vibrations, no creaky sounds. I immediately push the door open button, as I fully intended to jump off and take the stairs. I called out to the receptionist and she could hear me. The building super was being called. I just wanted off.

The elevator moved and when the door opened, I was staring at a concrete wall. Time to panic! The elevator continued to move for a second and then the door would open. Each time the view changed. I would see steel beams then more concrete walls. I could tell I was between floors. Coworkers were talking to me and that was helping me calm down a bit. The doors just kept opening and closing and I was really panicking. I didn't know what to do. Then it hit me, I lay down on the floor and closed my eyes. I was reciting the Lord's Prayer.

The next time the door opened I could see the fifth floor. I climbed up about nine or ten inches, crawled out and ran to my desk.

I was weak and shaking but very happy to be off that old elevator. The whole experience seems silly and funny now. Thank God I can laugh about it today. This little story may not compare to someone who has endured much harder struggles. Yet, this is just a simple reminder of how God works in our everyday life.

Barbara

My Story 19

"No one will be able to stand up against you all the days of your life. As I was with Moses, so I will be with you; I will never leave you or forsake you."
Joshua 1:5

3am, deserted shipyard, foreign country, small pickup truck. My officer in charge is much stronger than I thought. I realize I cannot fight him off. I have my m16 rifle within reach, but there is no way I can shoot him. Who would believe me? How could I live with killing someone and besides, there was no way to maneuver the rifle in the small cab, not in the position I was in. My mind is racing, he is talking crazy to me; calling me a different woman's name, apologizing while he continues to struggle with me. I am helpless. Everything this tough soldier thought she would do in this situation is useless. I start praying, I ask God to help me, to tell me what to do, to bring someone to this isolated place and walk up to the truck, to stop him; nothing happens... Then, I had an instant peace, my mind became clear, my fear left me. I remembered the words to an anonymous prayer I had memorized as a child:

> **I am never alone, God the Father is ALWAYS with me, my soul, my identity, that something that says "I am I" is an eternal gift from God. God has a great purpose in life me, which He is revealing day by day. In God's care, no harm can**

befall me. I give myself over to God's protection and I will follow His guidance day by day.

I knew God was with me, I knew I was not alone in this horrible moment. I stopped struggling, I spoke to the Major as if I was the woman he was calling me. He became less violent and stopped hurting me as much. I have wondered if I had not been able to gain some control of myself, if he would have killed me when he was done. No one would have ever found my body on that isolated island.

I have many deep scars from that night. At times, the memories take over me and take too much control and power over my life. All these years later and "what ifs" about that night still seep into my mind.

My prayer to be removed from that night, for things to have ended differently did not happen. Does that mean God deserted me? No! God had a plan for me then and He has a plan for me today. I do not know why this happened to me, but God does and I trust in Him. I felt His peace, I felt His love and it was ok… because I am never alone.

Tonya

MyStory 20

"...but be transformed by the renewing of your mind..."
Romans 12:2

"Accept one another, then, just as Christ accepted you, in order to bring praise to God."
Romans 15:7

"What's WRONG with you?" "You should be ashamed of yourself!" "You know better!" Have you heard or even said any of these words before?

Shame... It's not just a feeling. Sometimes people confuse shame with guilt. Guilt involves an action outside of oneself. Shame on the other hand is a belief. It's a mindset. It's a belief that something is inherently defective or wrong with you.

When someone has had the belief and mindset of shame they tend to hear phrases like these even when they are not spoken. You may say one thing but they totally hear another. They have a constant judge in their ear. Nothing they do is ever good enough. Acceptance and a sense of belonging do not exist.

Growing up I lived in a shamed-based system. Religion to me was all about the "do's & don'ts." If I did all the "right" things

I felt others and God would accept and love me. Belonging was an elusive concept I was never going to grasp or understand. Relationships didn't involve communication or a range of emotion. Needs were not expressed.

I don't often start conversation. I don't often know how to express a need. Emotions are hard for me to express when they are not apathy, anger, or depression. I tend to walk in a room and try to determine another person's moods or emotions and act accordingly based on what I've observed. I'm a people pleaser, a giver, and I don't know how to truly accept a gift or compliment without feeling like I must return it in some way.

All of this is a result of shame, that inherent feeling that there is something defective in me. "I couldn't possibly deserve anything good." "How could God possibly love and accept me with all that is wrong with me?"

God has been teaching me that shame is a "mind set." The thoughts and beliefs can be replaced with His Truth.

> *"If then you were raised with Christ, seek those things above, where Christ is, sitting at the right hand of God. Set your mind on things above, not on things on the earth. For you died and your life is hidden with Christ in God."*
>
> Colossians 3:1-3

No matter the messages of my past, God has told me: I am Accepted, I am Loved, and I Do Belong to Him. From the beginning He has believed that I am Wonderfully and

Beautifully made. He doesn't see me as defective. He sees me in Christ and therefore I am not defective. I may sin but I'm not defective. In Christ I can accept the gift of grace and no longer feel I have to return it. I now have a choice! God wants to communicate with me. He wants to know my needs and it's okay to express them to Him.

Amy

My Story 21

"When they saw the courage of Peter and John and realized that they were unschooled, ordinary men, they were astonished and they took note that these men had been with Jesus"

Acts 4:13

I hate school. I always have since I can remember. My mom thinks maybe I was traumatized at school thanks to a Pre-K teacher, but who knows. I had a gift of memorizing things and getting along with the other kids, but put work in front of me and I just couldn't do it. So from that point on I didn't care to be studious, go to college, etc. I ended up barely graduating high school and got a certificate in 4 months at a local community college.

As I watch my husband work his butt off to graduate college and perhaps pursue his masters, it gets me regretting that I hadn't cared about school. I hear my sisters, cousins, and friends talk about getting their degrees, living on campus, writing tons of papers, and strangely I get jealous. And honestly, I start to tear myself down. Many thoughts go through my head, like how stupid I am, how useless I am, how I'm nothing without a college degree. Shoot, I don't even have the ambition to get one. I wish I did, I truly do.

I recently started getting embarrassed when people ask where I got my degree from. So the more I thought about it, the more I just felt less than ordinary, less than anything. But then Acts 4:13 popped up in my daily reading, interrupting a pity party I was throwing for me. And it took me aback.

Peter and John were unschooled and ordinary, yet they had courage. People saw by their actions and words that they had been with Jesus and were living for Him. How amazing is that?! The men didn't look at their degrees, look back at what fraternity they were a part of, etc. It was such a relief to read that two of the greatest figures in the New Testament besides Jesus were, just like me, unschooled and ordinary. So if you're like me, don't put yourself down. Just because you don't have your degree in doctor neuro-physicist (or whatever smart thing everyone else has!) doesn't mean that God can't use you. I encourage you to remember that God used Peter and John, the unschooled and ordinary men. So whether you have a college education or barely graduated high school, or haven't graduated, I truly believe that God can and will use you to do great things. I am compelled to share this experience to help encourage and provide some hope as I have discovered the peace that surpasses all understanding with this struggle of mine.

Shaniqua

My Story 22

"He will swallow up death forever. The Sovereign Lord will wipe away the tears from all faces; He will remove the disgrace of His people from all the earth. The Lord has spoken. In that day they will say, "Surely this is our God; we trusted in Him, and He saved us. This is the Lord; we trusted in Him; let us rejoice and be glad in His salvation."

Isaiah 25:8-9

The Yearning

"There is a yearning in hearts weighed down by ancient grief and centuries of sorrow. A yearning for tomorrow."

Choir members were asked to pick one of the songs from the Singing Christmas Tree and tell what it means to them. Immediately, I knew which song had already touched me at rehearsals.

Some people yearn for bigger bank accounts, larger homes, and a new car or just yearn to be something different than they are.

My yearning was for a lost loved one. David had been born with a rare heart condition and wasn't supposed to survive the night. We were told that if he did live to be six years old, chances were he would never walk because the poor blood flow didn't give him enough oxygen to maintain a healthy life. He had his first heart surgery at two weeks old and many more to follow.

Not only did he walk, he attended school until his condition worsened and then worked for his GED and went to college for a semester. His desire was to be a normal man, in spite of his weakened condition, he pushed forward every day. There were years of hospital stays, surgeries and treatments, he never wavered in his faith in the Lord. David had no fear of dying that did make the news of needing a heart /liver transplant a little easier. At least until it happened.

To lose a child, has to be the worst feeling anyone can feel. The pain, the emptiness inside never leaves. There is a big hole in your heart. I wrote about this song because it says exactly what happens and what God can do; I knew in my heart that my son was much happier now. He had suffered way too long, so death, from this world was welcome.

Before David entered Chapel Hill Hospital for the Heart/Liver transplant, he told me, "Mom, I am so tired, I'm ready to go HOME"(HEAVEN)

He was "yearning" for a better life.

Weeks later I found myself "yearning" too. Yearning just to see my son one more time, yearning for one more hug. I couldn't sleep or eat. I prayed, trusting God to help me find comfort.

One of those sleepless nights, I had a visitor. My son came to my room and sat on the side of my bed. He put his arms around me "Mom", he said smiling, "everything is alright." I could feel his arms around me giving me the hug that I had so yearned for. I slept well that night and woke the next morning hungry.

"There is a yearning when ALL our sorrows are erased and we shall SEE the ONE who placed within our hearts the yearning."

What are you yearning for today? A lost loved one? Better health? A better job? Maybe a better relationship with God? Are you yearning for the PROMISED ONE?

PS

This is all true; it was no dream, no vision, and no imaginary thing from the mind. My son was as real sitting on the side of my bed as he was weeks before his surgery. God is so good! I am looking forward to seeing my son on "The Other Side of Heaven" one day.

Blessings,

Margaret

MyStory 23

> *"Then Peter came to Jesus and asked, "Lord, how many times shall I forgive my brother or sister who sins against me? Up to seven times?" Jesus answered, "I tell you, not seven times, but seventy-times seven."*
>
> Matthew 18:21-22

Everyone has THAT friend. The one who you would go crying to when someone wronged you, and to encourage you they would tell you "Just you wait honey, karma is coming. It'll get back to him". And whether you believed in karma or not, you would wait and watch on the sidelines, waiting for karma or something to kick him right in the behind. And then once karma got him and got him good, you could walk off with a little smile on your face, somehow wanting to write karma a thank you note for doing that to him.

But what happens when karma isn't fair?

That's what happened when I left my abusive ex-husband. I'd go crying to my girlfriends about all the things my "abusing, cheating, no good ex-husband" had done to me and that it just wasn't fair. They'd all let me cry while drinking too much wine and tell me not to worry, because karma is a bummer and was sure to be a big one to him after everything. Even my church friends would share their Godly piece on forgiveness and then reassure me about karma and telling me to wait, that I would see it! I didn't care if I believed in karma or not, I was excited! I could only plot in my head all the horrible things that would happen to him after all he had done to me.

But the days went on, and nothing seemed to happen. Days turned into weeks, weeks into months, etc. And from what I could gather from friends and Facebook stalking, nothing major happened. In fact, his life seemed to be ok. And as me being the great Christian woman, my first thought was "Praise the Lord!" Totally kidding. I wish that was the first thought! Instead I got angry, bitter, and even resentful.

Now don't get me wrong, I had forgiven him, or at least started that process as much as I could. I knew I had to forgive him to get over it, get into heaven, etc. But one morning as I was having a pity party that karma hadn't hit my ex with a semi-truck filled with pillows (including the pillows made me feel like a compassionate human being instead of one with anger issues. No judging allowed!), I read a bible story that I heard all my life. You know it, the one where Jesus says to forgive 70 times 7. I would always exclaim "Wow, that's a lot" and never think anything else of it.

But after reading Matthew 18:21-22 on this particular morning, suddenly it hit me (almost as hard as a semi-truck filled with pillows). Jesus didn't intend for us to forgive those who sinned against me all those times in just one sitting. Jesus, as a human, knew that pain from a sin done against you doesn't go away once you forgive them that first time. Forgiveness is defined "to stop feeling angry toward someone who has done something wrong". Forgiveness is being happy for the person who wronged you when their life is going well. Forgiveness is being ok when karma isn't vindictive. So years later, I have finally given up on karma and have put more time and effort into forgiving 70 times 7. Shoot, we might be past that number now. It's not easy, and sometimes my selfish side wishes karma would knock on my ex's door. But let's be real. Jesus has had to forgive me way more times then I'll probably ever have to forgive anyone, so I reckon it's worth a shot. And I'd rather be like Jesus and be a forgiver than be like karma and be a…well, you know.

Della

MyStory 24

> *"For the Son of Man came to seek and to save what was lost."*
>
> Luke 19:10

For as long as I can remember I have always been moved by epic stories. Stories of love, loss, trial, triumph, brokenness, and redemption. These are the kinds of stories that move you to stand up and fight for something bigger than yourself. Or hope for beauty and love that you are sure will find you one day. As is standard for most young girls growing up in America, I was born and bred on Disney princess movies. I ate them up, soaked them in and fantasized about being someone worthy to be rescued by a handsome prince. As I got older, my affections became more sophisticated and took the form of romantic comedies. I would love getting lost in the twist and turns of these awkwardly lovely stories. Stories that had a familiar predictability that provided strange solace to my soul. In some ways these romantic flicks emulated the Disney movies I watched as a young girl and went a little like this:

Girl is lonely, lost and feeling incomplete. She knows that something is missing and deduces that the missing piece is another person (preferably a man in the form of a prince on a white steed). Girl aimlessly wanders through life until through some serendipitous interaction she meets HIM, the man of her dreams (or obsessions, fantasies, etc.). She knows nothing about this elusive Mystery Man but to her he is perfect. He says all the right things, looks exactly the way she always imagined he would and becomes in her mind the ultimate Prince Charming. Of course it must be fate. As the hour and a half drama unfolds, something traumatic happens and tears the boy away from the girl and they are forced to part. The anguish on both sides is unbearable and you think it's all over until the forces of love bring them back together and they live happily ever after.

I think all of us would admit that deep down we love these stories. They are safe, predictable and in some ways hope giving. I loved getting lost in the made up lives of the movie characters I would watch. Their stories began to shape my expectations of how I thought my life would unfold. Little did I know those expectations and unchecked longings would have disastrous consequences.

Part 1: A deadly path cloaked in beauty

> *"There is a way that seems right to a man, but its end is the way to death"*
> —Proverbs 14:12 ESV

It was my senior year of high school; I was 17 and ready to take on the world. I couldn't wait to experience all that life had to offer. I always considered myself a fairly good kid, didn't get into much trouble, had plenty of friends and was a member of the Fellowship of Christian Athletes in school (even though I was the most uncoordinated girl you would ever meet), I had even said the "sinners prayer" when I was 10 years old and was proudly leaving high school with my virginity intact. Sure I had experimented sexually with guys I had dated but I was still technically a virgin and for that I was proud. All of that was about to change when I met a dark haired, blue eyed guy who I decided that I just had to date. I had in my mind that he was the answer to all of those longings that I so desperately needed filled. He would fulfill the role of my fairy-tale Disney prince, romantic comedy hero that I was searching for. I had only known him for a week but I gave him something that I now know was one of the most precious things I could ever give anyone. I gave him my heart and my virginity out of my desperation. He never spoke to me again after that night and I was devastated, ashamed and embarrassed. That one action sent me down a road of destruction and death that I never anticipated. Something deep inside me died and I began to build a wall up around the ache in my heart. Instead of running to the Lord, I went further and further down the road of destruction and began using men and food as my ointment of choice. I was blinded by my pain and that blindness led me to some dark places.

Part 2: Sin that led to death

> *"When tempted, no one should say, "God is tempting me." For God cannot be tempted by evil, nor does he tempt anyone; [14] but each person is tempted when they are dragged away by their own evil desire and enticed. [15] Then, after desire has conceived, it gives birth to sin; and sin, when it is full-grown, gives birth to death."*
>
> James 1:13-15

For three years of my life through college I ran hard after my desires which led to further heartbreak. I didn't know my right from my left and many times I remained in a fog of my own loneliness and pain. Through my hurt over broken relationships, I used food as an attempt to make the gnawing hurt go away. I developed an eating disorder that kept me in prison for almost 6 years of my life. At this point in my life, that prayer that was prayed to Jesus so many years ago in my small country church seemed to have no impact on my life. I didn't even know how to call out to this Jesus that felt so removed from my situation. Many nights I would just lie in my bed and cry longing to be rescued from the mess I knew I had gotten myself into. I thought I had gone much too far for even Jesus to help me and even though I knew He could, I didn't believe that He even wanted to. Three years into my mess, I met a woman named Stacy on my college campus that sat down with me and shared the gospel in a way that I had never heard it before. When I was a little girl, I was terrified of this God who would send me to hell if I didn't accept His Son. When I walked down my church aisle to proclaim my allegiance to Christ, I was more afraid of losing my eternal life than spending an eternal life with my Savior. It was at that moment that the Lord used Stacy in Part 3 of my life.

Part 3:

> *"But he was pierced for our transgressions, He was crushed for our iniquities; the punishment that brought us peace was on Him, and by His wounds we are healed."*
>
> —Isaiah 53:5

The moment Stacy read that verse to me, I burst into tears. I longed to know THAT Savior. He was a man that was worthy to give my whole being to. He was the one that my little girl heart longed for all those years I would fill my time watching love stories. As the old song goes, "I was looking for love in all the wrong places." But when I looked into the face of Love in the form of Christ that day my heart broke and I fully surrendered my life and felt peace like I had never felt before.

Now in saying all of this, I don't want to paint a picture that everything from that point on was perfect. I fought a 6 year battle with an eating disorder that he rescued me from just two years ago. I still had so much pain in my heart from my poor choices that he needed to redeem. In addition I have had to walk away from a few relationships that were not a part of His plan for me and there is still a sting in my heart over that. But my God can be trusted and I am currently in a season of asking Him to help me fall in love with Him through His word. He is the hope of my salvation. He alone. Of this I am confident:

> ...."*Being confident of this that he who began a good works in you will carry it on to completion until the day of Christ Jesus.*"
> –Philippians 1:6 NIV

> "*I will praise the LORD as long as I live; I will sing praises to my God while I have my being. Do not trust in princes, in mortal man, in whom there is no salvation. When his breath departs, he returns to the earth; on that very day his plans perish. Blessed is he whose help is in the God of Jacob,*

whose hope is in the LORD his God, who made heaven and earth, the sea, and all that is in them, who keeps faith forever; who executes justice for the oppressed, who gives food to the hungry. The LORD sets the prisoners free; the LORD opens the eyes of the blind. The LORD lifts up those who are bowed down; the LORD loves the righteous."

– Psalm 146:2-8 ESV

Mary Elizabeth

My Story 25

"Do not let your hearts be troubled, Trust in God and trust Me."

John 14:1

I don't know how some of these wives do it? Their husbands have Parkinson's, Alzheimer's, or Dementia. Their husbands can't do things around the house because of bad backs, bad knees or bad hearts. Yet these women are compassionate, carrying, have patience, are respectful and loving to their husbands. HOW? How can they not go crazy? Why are they not yelling at their husbands out of frustration? How come I can't be the good wife instead of the ugly one??

My husband retired early from his job to pursue a degree in Apologetics. We both felt the Lord leading us for this change and we were excited about being a team for Gods plans. Very nice and noble thinking! Things started out well and came together, just like people would say we are 'in Gods will'.

Then it began.

My husband went from an "A" student to failing classes. He was tired all the time. I would come home from work and he would still be in bed and not know what day it was. He wasn't able to concentrate enough to drive. He went from taking complete care of the house and yard to not having the strength to push up the garage door to get the mower.

Luckily we found out what was going on. He has a "non disease" called Chronic Lyme. We started going to DC for treatment. We found out that the CDC and the insurance companies do not recognize Chronic Lyme and do not pay for treatment. So, lots of medicines, lots of bills, and lot more of being sick.

We are in our 3rd year of his treatment. And I am failing as a wife. I do not come home from work full of compassion for my sick husband. I do not rush in the door and start a healthy, gluten free meal for him; I do not even want to talk to him since he is still in bed. How do these good wives do it? My poor husband feels horrible both mentally and physically. I know I am not helping him feel important, strong, or even close to being the "man of the house." I hear the tone in my voice when I talk to him sometimes and it makes me cringe. Just how hateful can I be? Why am I not treating him the way I see other wives care for their sick husbands?

Sometimes I feel justified in my treatment of him. I am tired, I am depressed, I am also now being treated for Chronic Lyme, I have to work even when I feel sick, I have lost the dreams of the future, I see my paycheck going to medical bills, I am in the mist of menopause... I.., I.., I.., I...I realize that when all I can think about is "I" I start feeling sorry for myself.

The Bible says Christ will give me rest, that God is the Great Physician, and that the Lord knows the plans for my future. I just need to trust God and let Him take the troubles of my heart.

I get peace in God's Word and promises. I know He is with me. At times I close my eyes and imagine Christ is holding me in His arms and letting me rest. I wish I could say I am the perfect wife to my sick husband now, but I am not. I continue to struggle with this every day. I am ashamed and embarrassed by my lack of compassion to my husband at times. I am praying that soon I will be able to relax and let God handle this mess. I need to let go of my control and give it to Him.

It all sounds so easy to do, but it's not. But I am going to keep trying. Maybe one day soon I will be the wife my husband needs. The wife that other women will look at and say…" I wish I could be like her". Or better yet, I will someday be the wife that God created me to be!

Sarah

My Story 26

"But godliness with contentment is great gain"
1 Timothy 6:6

For me, godliness can come easily at times. But godliness with contentment? That is something that I realized I don't do very well with. And that's my own fault.

When I was younger I fed all the temptations I desired, over and over and over again. It was a sinful rush that I loved, and it was fun being the cute bad girl.

Eventually I wondered why I would expect God to bless me if I wasn't living my life right. For example, if you needed a lung transplant but you were smoking, do you think someone would trust you with a new pair of healthy lungs? That answer is no. In the same way, why would the Lord want to give you a gift if He sees you continually ignoring and messing up the gifts and blessings He's already given you?

Praise the Lord I found my way back to Him, but that didn't mean that I was content with godliness. To this day, I still struggle with being content in my godliness. There are days that I would rather be out getting drunk and dancing on a bar than watching Jeopardy in my pajamas. There are nights I would rather be flirting with a soon to be one night stand than cuddling with my amazing husband that is snoring off into sweet dreams. There are many other words I'd rather say than "ah heck".

But I love choosing the latter, I really do! I get so much more joy living with God in my heart, and living that out in my life. Every day I strive to be content with my godliness, and each day it gets more comfortable and natural feeling. I am continuously blessed in my life because I choose to be content with my godliness, even though it's not always easy or my first choice. And that joy I now have in my life beats any sinful rush that I experienced before. It is truly a great gain to be content with godliness.

Emily

MyStory 27

"He sent forth His word and healed them; He rescued them from the grave."

Psalm 107:20

I am grateful for my story… the good, the bad, the ugly… This doesn't mean that I'm happy with all the events that have taken place in my life, and it doesn't mean I wouldn't change anything if I could. Nor does it mean I don't feel regret at times about my past…it simply means I accept it for what it is and I'm willing to move on.

That's the point, moving on.

I've found I can't adequately do this without owning my life in its totality. If I only acknowledge the good stuff and dismiss all the pain, claim only my accomplishments and deny my failures, if I only share my joy and bury my sorrow; I would never be whole or feel complete. I would never be real and if I can't get real, I can't heal or move on. I am the sum total of every moment I've experienced in life.

In my quest for spiritual maturity it's become clear the events that have taken place in my life have served as a catalyst for change. Often I was resistant to the change and in the midst of my circumstances it was difficult to move into a state of transition. But once there I was forced to make a choice; I could try to deny the state I was in, I could try to escape where I was, I could focus on finding someone or something to blame for whatever the situation was in my life or I could surrender and find my way through it. I wish I could say I always chose the latter. I could've saved myself a whole lot of heartache and time wasted, but often it takes a certain amount of resistance before surrendering to really understand the benefits of letting go.

Today I'm grateful for the choices I've made, I'm grateful for my days of denial, I'm grateful for my attempts to escape reality, I'm grateful for the times I was mad at the world and blamed all my problems on how unfair and unjust it was! I'm grateful for the times when I was just rebellious and refused to acknowledge anything was wrong, especially with me, trying to create an illusion that everything was just fine. In looking back and reflecting on my life story, I have to remind myself that I did the best I could with what I had to work with at any given time. What I realize now is with each experience, I had a little more to work with, thanks to the time before. Through it all I can see how every experience is woven together into the person I am today.

If I deny my weaknesses, then I have to deny my strengths, if I deny ever making mistakes, then I deny my humanness, and if I deny any part of my story, then I deny my claim to victory! I'm thankful in ALL circumstances, because it's through them where true transformation has taken place within me. I'm grateful I can 'Walk MY Talk' today because it's in that walk I've learned to accept where I came from, understand where

I've been, and embrace where I am now. Life has molded me into who I am and I know I didn't do it by myself.

Through every step along the way I had the hands of the masterful potter helping to shape and create me into all He would have me be. I'm just an ordinary woman with an extraordinary God! I'm grateful to finally understand my life is my story and I do have some say so about the character I play in it. I can be an active participant in my life today. My story is a gift because it represents life and I wouldn't have a story to share if it were not for God's loving grace and blessed mercy in my life today. God is the author of my life and together we are writing a beautiful story. Living peacefully, loving freely, and forgiving faithfully, because it's my story and I choose to live it gratefully.

Lynda

My Story 28

"Is any one of you in trouble? He should pray..."
James 5:14

"Be joyful always; pray continually; give thanks in all circumstances for this is God's will for you in Christ Jesus."
1 Thessalonians 5:16-18

"He will take great delight in you, he will quiet you with his love, he will rejoice over you with singing."
Zephaniah 3:17

As I look back over my life what stands out most is how God provided the right scripture at the right time. Hebrews 4:12a states *"For the Word of God is living and active."* This has surely proved true in my life. There are four scriptures that come to mind when I reflect on this.

The first situation was when my daughter, Allison, was facing open heart surgery at 11 months old. The elders of the church called her dad and I to the church to lay hands over her, pray and anoint her with oil. This was a new concept for me as I grew up in a church that did not do that. James 5:14 says, "Is any one of you sick? He should call the elders of the church to pray over him and anoint him with oil in the name of the Lord." It was a powerful moment which ended up giving me a peace as we approached this surgery. It helped me realize whether she lived or died she was in God's hands. My role was just to love her and be there for her. God brought us through and she is an adult now. Praise God!

"Be joyful always; pray continually, give thanks in all circumstances, for this is God's will for you in Christ Jesus." 1 Thessalonians 5:16-18. Really, God, is this what you expect of me, going through divorce? It was the beginning stages of my divorce proceedings and I was crying all the time. The sermon that Sunday morning was about being joyful always. After church we went home, had lunch and I was sitting outside watching my three children play. As the warm sun was beating down on me it came to me that my children needed to experience the joy in their lives. It helped me to get myself together and start making the best out of this awful situation.

Later in life scripture from Isaiah 43: 1-7 stands out to me. He has created me, redeemed me, and summoned me by name. He is always with me. The troubles I face in life will not destroy me. I am precious and honored in His sight. He loves me. I do not have to live in fear. God is right by me side no matter what I am going through and will bring me through to the other side. I struggle with liking myself and knowing the value God puts on me but this scripture tells me I am precious and honored in God's sight.

I will end with *"The Lord God is with you, He is mighty to save. He will take great delight in you, He will quiet you with*

Andrea Leffew

His love, He will rejoice over you with singing." Zephaniah 3:17. The reason that this scripture means so much to me is that God is singing over me. Wow!

Wendy

My Story 29

"But the fruit of the Spirit is love, joy, peace, patience, kindness, goodness, faithfulness, gentleness and self-control. Against these things there is no law."
Galatians 5:22

All Scripture speaks of being fruitful and multiplying. Even women who earnestly prayed and sacrificed had a child. Why do all the stories have a happy ending while mine was not? Every month, attempting to be hopeful, I'd invariably sit crying and asking God to let this pass over me so I could accept and cling to His will, not mine. I would attempt to pull it together and try again, month after month, for more than two years realizing that I was going from 35-37 and the pressure was mounting.

I would appease myself that during that two year period, my husband and I were traveling for work making our effort all the more challenging. That time transitioned from love making to baby making with a rigid schedule. None of which helped the situation. And, although, I was excited to hear about pregnancies, attend baby showers and witness baby dedications, my heart and body ached while tears stung my face. Sometimes, I would sit and sob. My thoughts and emotions were captive; especially on those special days and starting day. I was really feeling so lonely in a deep way!

I tried planting and gardening. I tried reading numerous books. I redecorated our kitchen. We tried artificial insemination. We were fortunate enough to have insurance and tried twice. Nothing, no hint of a pregnancy – no questionable pregnancy tests, nothing! Looking back, I am so thankful that I was raised to believe in a loving, living God who wants a relationship with me for all parts of my life. That HE knits us together in our mother's womb and numbers the hairs on our head (Luke12:7). I knew it was all up to HIM. Surely, He had a plan for me and this…didn't He? I decided I needed a women's bible study, a way for God to encourage me and speak to me about it all!

The bible study was on the Fruit of the Spirit and moved all throughout the bible in great depth each week for months. Of course, there was that one lady. You know the type, 'well if you'd only pray' (right, of course). Her well-intended words of encouragement (I hope – I only met her once) only hit me and made me feel worse. Didn't she know I WAS praying??!! My attention continued to focus more on Him and the gift of His counselor, the seal upon my faith. I immersed myself and our home. I stenciled the fruit of the Spirit words around the soffit of our kitchen. I dwelt on His words in my mind and in the hearth/soul of our home.

And, as I began to dig deep into the study of His word, He softened my heart and emotions day by day, week after week, month by month. His Counselor which was exactly what HE knew I needed. Funny, looking back on the study it was a month for each fruit or roughly 9 months. God took me through a season. And, boom, there it was in print, just a chapter before. Why had I not seen it or read it previously?

Be glad, o barren woman, who bears no children (Galatians 4:16). Right there in print! Yes, yes, I know that it is referencing an unmarried or widowed woman (Isaiah 54:1 *Sing o barren woman*) but still He spoke to me, right to my soul – I was not alone! He spoke to me and encouraged me that my work is in the Spirit not in the Earthly flesh realm. Right then, I decided to give up trying and we stopped short of in-vitro. For me, I realized that God has so many children in need of love. They are merely arrows that He puts into a parent's quiver for a short time with the goal of aiming and shooting them back to Him. They are His and really didn't need to come from my womb. How, He longs for children. He lovingly and patiently waits. Wow, what a revelation…why had it taken so long! I accepted His will!

A few years later, at 42, I was having a pretty tough and unusual menstruation. I went to the doctor since it was much heavier than normal. The nurse walked into the room and said it's positive. What…I've got diabetes?! Both my grandfather's had diabetes and it's inherited, so I'm always alert to it. She smiled and said your pregnancy test is positive but you're having a miscarriage. I was in shock…how did I not know I was pregnant or miscarrying. We hadn't used any type of birth control that entire time thinking it just wasn't possible. How far I had traveled emotionally and mentally? After the initial shock wore off, I smiled and sensed that God was reassuring me that my body was fine, healthy and that with Him all things are possible. HE was also affirming/confirming His plan for my life. My husband invited me into the backyard to share a short and beautiful time to say goodbye and acknowledge the miscarried baby's spirit who would not suffer here on this Earth but stayed with God, in His presence. How comforting that time and imagery was for me! I am so thankful to him and to God for that moment.

I grew to see any baby as such a Holy Gift! And, there are many gifts. The more I embraced His truth the more love, joy, peace, patience, kindness, goodness, faithfulness, gentleness and self-control I've found. That scripture has and continues to sustain me in all kinds of ways and trials. He has a plan for my life, a plan to love His creation - children of all ages, sizes and shapes. Children/people who can be free (freedom in Christ) and not slaves to sin (or emotions) to be reunited with their Father! I am so blessed and thankful to have two step-children who I truly see as God's gift to me. I am able to celebrate and rejoice when I hear of a pregnancy, attend a baby shower or witness a baby dedication. I still occasionally shed a tear but now it's for the opportunity to see the majesty and mystery of God's gifts and pray that child too will know and love Him! To God be the Glory for the Great Works He has done!

Tammy

My Story 30

"Be joyful in hope, patient in affliction, faithful in prayer."

Romans 12:12

The title of my story should really be "How I Stopped Crying".

When my daughter was diagnosed with an incurable chronic disease at the age of 23, I felt like I was hit by a brick building. I couldn't breathe. That was a year ago and looking back I can see how God helped me.

I did cling to Christ. I believe that all the people who helped me were angels sent by God. I don't think anything happens by coincidence because it's all God's design. I felt alone in my terrified state of emotions, but every human experiences suffering and we're never alone. I can now see God helping me in the angels he has put in my path. My mantra was (and still is) *"Be joyful in hope, patient in affliction, faithful in prayer."* Romans 12:12.

My daughter suffered for ten years prior to her diagnosis. We went to many different doctors and had hundreds of tests done. She had surgery to remove a baseball size cyst that we now believe was filled with Lyme disease. She hadn't slept through the night in five years. She lives in pain. We spent an entire day at the emergency room because she was suffering with chest pain and heart palpitations. After all the tests came back "ok", so the doctor gave her a valium and told her to go home and relax. At that point she did have a positive test for Lyme disease but the ER doctor told us that no doctor in North Carolina would treat her for Lyme. We were in such a desperate state and the events that led us to seek treatment in Washington, DC were by God's design.

We look at life differently now. The promise of eternal life in heaven with God is closer. Instead of giving each other a new shirt for birthday gifts we try to create memories for each other. It's the gift of spending time together. The memories of good days together will last a lifetime.

Vanna

My Story 31

"The LORD makes His face shine upon you and be gracious to you; the LORD turns His face toward you and gives you peace."

                                                     Numbers 6: 25-26

I talk to God though my prayers. When I turn to Him for help I do not always find the answers I want but if I accept, I find peace.

For example; when my son Michael married a woman who did not like his family. She turned him away from all of us. My heart was broken. Michael and his wife were cruel to the family at a time when we needed Michael's support the most. I did not know what to do. I spent days in prayer and asking for the answer. God's loving answer came, telling me to accept and love my son, to forgive him and his wife for the pain they have caused but let them go.

Remembering Numbers 6:25-26

"The LORD makes his face shine upon you and be gracious to you; the LORD turns his face toward you and gives you peace." I gave my pain to Him and I found peace".

Andrea Leffew

I found peace and kept Michael and his family in my prayers. Life can be hard but with faith and prayer, you can find comfort and lots of joy. I know you cannot do it alone you need prayer and God's help.

Carole

My Story 32

"For God so loved the world that he gave his one and only Son, that whoever believes in him shall not perish but have eternal life."

- John 3:16

I was born and raised in Africa. I attended college in Bong County, Africa; that is where I met my ex-husband, James. I had to cook and sell food to fellow students on the weekends in order to purchase basic day-to-day needs. I purchased these items for James and me. Like my family, his family was unable to provide him with the basic necessities he needed. We dated during our entire collegiate career, four years.

The first time James cheated was with a fellow dorm mate, she lived across the hall from me. After I confronted him about the infidelity, he was very remorseful. I did not think he would ever cheat on me again. After we graduated, I became pregnant. James was obtaining his Master's degree when we found out we were going to have our son. I flew to America so that we could get married before the baby was born. I went back to Africa so that I could give birth to our son. James graduated from the University and went back to Africa. Three years later, we were living a seemingly normal and happy life, I was pregnant with our second child, and we had very good jobs. Everything was fine until I heard he was dating a woman that lived in our neighborhood. After I confronted him, he did not deny that he was seeing the woman. He asked me to forgive him, so I forgave him. I felt as if he was very sorry and remorseful for what he did. I felt as if he truly loved me, because I had never really been loved by anyone before; I did not understand what true love really was.

About five years later, the civil war in my country started; we had to leave our homes and everything we owned behind. Luckily, James received an invitation to continue his studies at the university, from his former professor. The family: my two kids, two nieces and myself, were able to come to the United States with James. While he continued to his education, I worked to support the family.

After his graduation from the university, we moved to SC. When we moved he was still studying for his CPA license. During that time, he and his cousin opened up their own business. I was working four jobs to compensate the income. About a year after the business opened it failed, and we were $20,000 in debt.

All my life I did everything for everyone else, my children were in college and James had a good paying job. I felt as if it was time for me to do something for myself, so in 2005, I decided to continue my education. I started nursing school while working full time; I failed. So, I decided to go all in and only work part-time; James was furious. He claimed we did not have enough money for me to only work part time. Thinking back, I am happy I did not listen to him. I did not know he was using my income to support his cheating habit.

A few years later James asked me for a divorce. I asked him why he wanted a divorce and he told me that he simply wanted "out" of our marriage. I was devastated. We were still living together at the time; I woke up one night and heard James on the phone. I heard him talking to his mistress of three years, "May". May was also married with a child. They were discussing me that night; I was shocked to say the least. When I asked him about it he said, "Don't make such a big deal, you know the marriage is over". The veil was lifted from my eyes; I started to "get smart" when it came to our marriage. I started to look through all our finances and phone records. I found out that he was taking her on trips and more while I was in school and working. After the phone incident, he started sleeping out of the house. We decided to live in the house together so that we could fix it up and sell it.

One day, James was cleaning the gutters and I was holding the ladder. I started thinking about all the things he has done to me and everything he had put me through, I almost pulled the ladder from under him. The only thing that saved his life was God. I thought about what God would want me to do and what my children's lives would be like. In that moment, I decided to leave. I knew God had helped me through nursing school, so that I could help others.

It was only through God's grace and mercy, that I became a practicing nurse. God brought me through all the "drama"; he loved me through all my wicked thoughts, his kindness, and his unconditional love for me. God gave me what I needed when I needed it. I am thankful and I will always praise his name.

Edith

MyStory 33

"Do not be anxious about anything, but in everything, by prayer and petition, with thanksgiving, present your requests to God. And the peace of God, which transcends all understanding, will guard your hearts and your minds in Christ Jesus."
Philippians 4:6-7

I know it's crazy and almost like self-torture, but I think about my daughters' future. How can I not?? Will it be painful, slow, drown out, will they hate me for giving them the Cystic Fibrosis? Will they feel peace and not be afraid?

As my daughters have grown and lived past their original CF life expectancy, I wait nervously for the next "expiration date" to come. I know this fear is not a healthy way to live and it will make me crazy. So I keep these fears stuffed deep in my heart. They are painful to think about and will ruin my facade of functioning normally. People will ask "how ya doing?" I want to scream "like crap!" My daughters are sick, all of them. Statistically I will bury my daughters and my parents sometime within the next 10 years. But instead, I say I am fine and smile.

I feel better at work when I am able to help people, to keep my mind off my future. The experiences I've had with my daughters' health issues have made me more compassionate and realistic in my work. I truly "know what they are going through". This helps to take my focus off of my life for a while and look for joy in the day.

But honestly, I am so afraid of the future. I am so afraid of the pain of losing my daughters. At times it will slip out of my locked heart and I will cry. I will think about their dreams being taken away and I will cry. I wonder if I will ever be a grandmother and I cry. Have I already mourned enough? Will this make it easier if the time comes? I doubt it. How can burying a child for any reason be easy?

How have I kept from not totally cracking up and becoming a useless pile of self-pity? I hang on to the heels of Jesus! His words and His promise give me peace when reality gets to painful. *"And the peace of God which transcends all understanding will guard your heart and minds in Christ Jesus."* Philippians 4:7. If I turn my focus on Christ, He guards my heart.

I do not know how I will react if the day comes that CF takes my daughters away. I do know that I will not be alone. No matter how much pain my heart will feel, Christ will be there to keep it from breaking.

Andrea

My Story 34

"A cheerful heart is good medicine, but a crushed spirit dries up the soul"
                                              Proverbs 17:22

I love my job! I get to see miracles and I meet all kinds of people from all areas of life. I am truly blessed with the career I am in. It's the field that I feel God gave me gifts and talents to be used in. But oh, there are days, Oh my gosh, there are days!! Sometimes I want to say every horrible thing in my head, get in my car and drive until I run out of gas!!

Another day of smiling, listening and encouraging. I just don't think I have it in me anymore! Every day, I go into strangers home, families whose lives have been changed by illness of some kind. Their future changed forever. They look to me to give them some hope. Some expect me to be able to give them their past back. I listen to the wives, husbands and children. I listen to the patients, all tell me of the pain, the fear, and the anger they feel. I hear folks talk of how unfair this illness/disease/accident has been to them. Sometimes I want to scream "ENOUGH! Life stinks, move on!!" Sometimes I can't help but want to call them whiney and weak, and tell them to get over it and move on! What can I do for them, I am not God! Do they realize that things could be much worse? Do they know I just left a home where cancer is spreading faster than the x-rays can keep up? Do they know there is a daughter who is trying to keep her mother out of a nursing home, but it is also destroying her marriage? Do they know that even though I am smiling and encouraging, I have defiant teenagers at home, my husband has not been able to find a job and hasn't worked for 4 years? Do they realize my back hurts, my knees ache and that I am about to have a hot flash?!?!

What do I do? I can't yell at people and call them names. That never goes over well! I would never just disappear (even though that sounds good sometimes). So, I take my own advice. I pull up my bootstraps, and ask God to give me the words, the strength, and the ability needed for each situation I walk into. I remember Proverbs 17:22 "A cheerful heart is good medicine, but a crushed spirit dries up the soul".

These families do not need another discouraging person in their lives. I know I cannot fix them, nor can I change their past, but I can be an encouraging smile, a cheerful heart, maybe a shoulder to cry on. I am a drill sergeant in scrubs who helps them find their new "normal" in this life.

Sometimes the days and demands are just too long for me and I have nothing left. I feel like everything is squeezed out of me and that life is really rotten sometimes. But then I remember the people that I saw that day, the ones struggling with the death of their dreams, and how a simple encouraging word and smile brought them a little bit of hope. I see how the faith in Salvation can give hope in the midst of pain. I remember that I have been blessed to be part of such a raw part of someone's life. I remember it is not a job, but a responsibility to be a small part of Christ in their lives. This is what keeps my spirit from being crushed and dried up!

Vicki

My Story 35

"Do not hide your face from me, do not turn your servant away in anger; you have been my helper. Do not reject me or forsake me, God my Savior."
                                             Psalm 27:9

I guess my story starts when I was about eight. My parents had just divorced and my mom was getting ready to marry the man that I now call daddy. I was basically raised in the church. I don't even remember a time when we didn't go. I accepted Jesus as my Lord and Savior at a young age, probably the same time as when the parents divorced. I don't even remember much about accepting Jesus. I had to take a class, and then got baptized.

I pretty much cruised through life. It was easy and simple. I was a sheltered, naïve, innocent, and very happy young girl. We went on mission trips, choir trips, and retreats with our youth group. I always knew that God was with me and would be forever. Over the years that changed.

Right before I turned 18, I met a boy. It makes me feel so stupid and stereotypical to know that a boy completely changed my life, but it is what it is. I had just started college, was living with my sisters, and pretty much on my own for the first time.

I met Jack at the church I was raised in. We were in the same Sunday school class. Like normal, we started out as friends. He was new to my city, a few years older than me, going to divinity school, and had plans to be a chaplain in the Navy.

Our first date is one I will never forget. He was doing a paper for school and I was the subject since I have Cystic Fibrosis (CF) and was recently put on IV antibiotics. I don't remember exactly what we did before we started working on the paper, but we went out to eat and as he interviewed me, I became insanely itchy and knew something was wrong. The minute I got home I had my sisters check my sides and I had enormous hives. A few days later I was back in the hospital because of allergic reactions to the medicines that I was on.

The next few months were difficult for me. I continued to get hives, and couldn't really work. School was hard as I was in and out of the hospital. Jack stuck with me the whole time. I never had someone be with me throughout all of my CF stuff. Needless to say I fell pretty hard.

He told me he loved me within a few weeks of us dating, and we shared our first kiss in the hospital. This said a lot to me, because when you're in the hospital you don't exactly look your best. I was sure that this was it; I had met the man of my dreams.

At first, things went very smoothly for us. My parents liked him, my sisters liked him, and I was going to get a chance to meet his family for Christmas. I remember there being a lot of talk of marriage and us getting engaged over Christmas. I also remember that we had talked about marriage, but I did not think that we were going to get engaged. The holidays were great, but when we got back everything started to fall apart. I remember being so upset when we got back, not because we weren't engaged, but because it seemed like it was so important to my family that we weren't engaged. The next few months were very hard. There were a lot of fights between Jack and me, and a complete falling out with my family.

I chose Jack over my family. I moved with Jack to his home on the outskirts of Pittsburgh, PA for the summer. We were working on our relationship but he was proving he was not a very Godly or decent man. However, I was convinced I was in love and thought that we could get through anything. Once the summer ended our relationship basically did as well. For a supposed man of God, he did a lot of ungodly things.

After we broke up I did not know how to deal with it. I was alone. My family was gone, Jack was gone, I was homeless, depressed, and without any hope. My church family chose sides. The people that had helped raise me and guide me in my Christian faith, chose sides. I reached out to God and it felt like He wasn't there. My church family was gone, and therefore, it felt like God was gone.

I fell into a dark place. I moved in with my biological father and started hanging out with friends that were major partiers, so I started partying. This went on for about a year. I slowly started to heal. I worked my way out from under my ex-boyfriend. He had a tight grip on me for long after we broke up. Once I was able to get away from him, I was able to start healing my heart. I slowly picked myself up and put the pieces back together. My mother and I started to fix our relationship. I knew that I would never be the person I was before, but I was working on becoming a person that I no longer hated, one that I could love and was proud of.

Even though I was healing, I still was lost spiritually. I couldn't go to church without breaking down in complete anger. I did not want to talk or even hear about Jesus. He had abandoned me when I needed Him most, and there was no forgiving that. I was so hurt and angry still.

Why would He abandon me? Why would God let such a bad man hurt me? I had never doubted Him; I served Him. But now I was a hypocrite. I felt like a hypocrite. I hated anything to do with church.

I honestly do not know when all of that started to change. I started to let go of the anger. I was still hesitant about church, but I wasn't as opposed to it. I started going anytime I went to visit my parents, and stopped hating on church when I was home. This whole healing process took about four years.

I still am on my journey of healing. I know now that God had His hand on my healing. I know that because my mother and dad are people of faith, and that they never stopped praying for me. I still have my doubts, and still haven't found a church, or even a regular place that I can talk to God. God knows I doubt more than I believe. But there is hope now and I know it's not something I will find on my own. My relationship with God will never be as innocent as it was, but I think I am on my way to having a new relationship with Him again.

Amara

My Story 36

"Because of the Lord's great love we are not consumed, for His compassions never fail. They are new every morning; great is your faithfulness."
Lamentations 3:22-23

"*This is my story, this is my song. Praising my Savior, all the day long;*" That is part of a verse in a choral work of John Beck's "Assurance", and it became my mindset to help me cope with a lifetime of pain. My Jesus is the only medicine that has helped and He is the only doctor that knew what was wrong with me! The pain was unbearable and the time span I am speaking of was over ten years. Ten years is a lifetime when you are the one in the bed with pain. It becomes a life sentence when you must look in the eyes of your sweet children and dear husband, and see the anguish you put there.

Let me explain how my house of cards fell down around me. I was a devoted mom, wife, and an intensive care nurse. When I was a teenager, I dedicated my life to God and felt the call to be a medical missionary. Due to the icy roads one night, there was a shortage of nurses and I worked a double shift. That evening I was driving home in my little sports car when a moving van stopped in my path. He backed over my car fracturing my back in several places. I also had at that time osteoporosis, degenerative disk bone disease and Raynaud's syndrome. With the new fractures, this became the perfect storm for the Reflex Sympathetic Dystrophy (RSD) that put me in my bed for 10 years.

RSD pain is not pain like post-operation pain or even like child birth pain; it is much more than that! It would induce vomiting and I would go for days on end without sleeping. I truly wanted to die. My whole body would go into spasms and I would black out, sometimes for hours. One time my husband found me on the kitchen floor and I was blue and cold to the touch. I had been there for 4-6 hours and he did not think I was alive! This would happen again and again.

Year after year I saw my life go by. I saw my beautiful girls grow up without me. I would try to get up but it would take hours just to shower and get dressed because of pain. I ended up weighing over 330 lbs. which only added to my physical and mental pain. The most debilitating pain of all was the pain I would see on the faces of my family. I never wanted to hurt them, yet I had.

Doctors thought it was all in my head and would not take a good look at me. One day my husband, Bob, happened to see (I'm sure by God) on TV information about a new spinal catheter and pump implanted into the abdomen to manage severe pain. I had all but given up on going to doctors by then.

I had been given very poor treatment by some and even dangerous treatment by others. Yet I knew God was saying to me *"Because of the Lord's great love we are not consumed, for His compassions never fail...great is Your faithfulness"* (Lamentations 3:22-23). His blessed ASSURANCE!

After ten years of being overlooked, I met a doctor in Winston-Salem NC and he sent me to the Mayo clinic. They found that things were not in my head, but by now so much damage to my body had been done. The doctor did the pump and I gradually got back on my feet. I was 330 lbs. and bedridden for ten years, but that first day the pump provided some pain control. I got down on my knees and thanked God for blessing me with a second chance! I promised God if He would help me, I would get out of bed every day, make up my bed, stay out of bed, and praise Him the rest of the day. A promise I still keep today. It is just as sweet this morning as it was then!

God is so GOOD! I took baby steps to start getting well. I could only walk from my bed to my chair, and then to the living room, and slowly, after time I could walk to my mailbox. I then lost over 150lbs. Keep walking, smiling, singing, and keep praising my Lord!

GREAT IS HIS FAITHFULNESS!

Marie

My Story 37

"Finally, be strong in the Lord and in His mighty power."

Ephesians 6:10

THIS LIFE WITH MS HAS PURPOSE

I was diagnosed with Multiple Scoliosis (MS), in 1979. For more than 20 years I had mild symptoms.

But in 2001, I had a terrible time with new symptoms. I now had sharp nerve pain in my legs and back. Worse than that, I got vertigo. The vertigo was not just a little off-balance. Vertigo made my world go round and round whenever I moved. I was stuck in the bed, lying face down, for three months. I drank Ensures with a straw from the edge of the mattress.

Then I was hospitalized for the doctors to see if there was a cause for the vertigo. After testing with the ears and everything else, my neurologist concluded that the vertigo was caused by the MS. Further, he told me that it was probably **a permanent** condition. That was the worst kind of discouraging words.

The next day some friends were visiting and they said they would like to pray for me. Our daughter Lynn was there, too.

When they prayed, it was such a different experience. It was like God was in the room. I don't know how to explain it, but the room was as if "lit up" to us.

Two mornings later, when the nurse came in the morning, she did her usual – help me roll over from my stomach to my back. But all of a sudden, everything was different. The room was not turning round and round. The nurse pushed the bed control button to bring the head of the bed up a few inches. Gradually she got me all the way to sitting up in bed. The vertigo was totally gone! Thank you Lord! A little bit later my neurologist came by on his morning rounds. When he saw me he jumped in disbelief. I told them that **a miracle** had happened! (And he agreed by scratching his head.)

During the three months of being in bed, I had lost much of my mobility. That meant I needed rehabilitation. Nevertheless, I was happy to be anywhere without the vertigo that had taken over my life. It was like I had been given a whole new world.

In the rehab unit, every morning I was seated in line next to a woman who was grumbling and complaining all the time. Nobody wanted to be next to her. I tried talking to her, but she was inconsolable. I learned a lesson from her. I needed to quit the grumbling about the mobility I lost, and move on in life.

I learned to be THANKFUL. God gave me a miracle, and I knew in my heart that it was for a purpose. It was to get going and continue to serve as leader of the MS Christian Fellowship, a support group we started in 1991. It was so great to be without vertigo!

Andrea Leffew

The example of the apostle Paul hits home with me. He suffered many things in prison and elsewhere, yet all the more, they drove him WITH JOY to his purpose of spreading the gospel. And God was not punishing him through suffering. God was giving Paul a sense of urgency and humility that gave him an effective ministry. Paul said in Ephesians 6:10 –*"Finally, be strong in the Lord and in His mighty power."*

In 2002, I was able to have eight women come to my home, where we had a book study. We identified our spiritual gifts, and discussed the different ways that God had called us. I learned that my gift was encouragement, and this confirmed my calling to serve others with MS.

One of these women is the co-leader of the support group, and she kept the group going when I had vertigo and was in the hospital. There were four of us who started the group in 1991, and it is still meeting 23 years later with about 30 people attending

My husband, Herb, was so great during all the days of vertigo and hospital rehab. He was an encourager to me during the time when I was struggling with the nerve pain and the medicines that made me too sleepy to accomplish anything. We found better solutions.

Romans 8:28 speaks to me: *"Now we know that in all things God works for the good of those who love him, who have been called according to his purpose."*

Barbara H.

My Story 38

'But I trust in your unfailing love; my heart rejoices in your salvation. I will sing to the Lord, for He has been good to me."

Psalm 13: 5-6

My life changed forever in 1996. It was the year I had graduated from high school and was planning the next steps of my future. It was the year I was to start my own life. It was the year I watched my mother die.

My childhood was what most people would call dysfunctional. My parents were both addicts, but had been clean since I was 7. My parents had just recently divorced and both had returned to their addictions of alcohol and cocaine. My brother had stayed with my father and I was living with my mother. I was able to overlook much of my family's dysfunction because of my love for my parents.

When my parents divorced, I always had a fear of what I might find at home with my mom. My mother's 'boyfriend' was a drug dealer. I never knew if my mom would be strung out, what kind of people would be there buying drugs or if she would even be there. Sometimes she would be gone for days. It was sad to see my parents who had worked so hard to stay clean, fall back into the heartbreaking lifestyle of addiction.

I was gone a few weeks after graduating high school and I came home to find my mother very sick. She was sleeping all the time and unable to get out of bed. My first thought was that she got ahold of some bad drugs. I was not sure what to do at first because if I took her to the doctors they may arrest her due to drugs in her system. I tried to find out what she may have taken from her boyfriend, but of course he would have nothing to do with it. After a few days of my mom not getting better I took her to the doctors. They ran some test but sent her home. She continued to get worse. I really became scared when she was unable to eat or speak. I was afraid and called my aunt to ask for help. My mother was so weak; it took both of us to get her into the car to the hospital.

I was only 18 years old at the time and I was scared. My world was spinning and I felt I had nothing solid to grab to slow the spin down. The doctors ran all kinds of test on my mother but with no results. They asked about my mom's drug history and started to check for HIV. I didn't want to let my family know what was going on, but since she was still so sick, I started making calls. That evening, a surgeon came in and quickly told me the results. My mother had a mass in her brain surrounded by fluid and if he did not do surgery that night, the swelling may kill her by morning. He said it was a good thing I had brought her to the hospital when I did, otherwise she might be dead by morning.

The next two weeks were the longest in my life. My family was with me while they did many surgeries on my mother. My mother had her last surgery on September 11th, 1996. The doctors had said they could do no more for her. I was driving to the hospital that morning, and will not forget the peace I felt. It was a quiet drive, no traffic and I just knew the surgery would be a success and my life would return to that of a normal 18 year old, planning for my future. I was not prepared for seeing the surgeon walk towards me after surgery. I knew instantly it was not good news. He said they had done all they could and I had to make the decision of either radiation or no treatment. Radiation could keep her sick and maybe live for 6 months, or no treatment and die in a few months. I still remember today the pain I felt as I fell to the ground screaming "No". This was my mother, my best friend, the women who taught me so much about life and love, and she had just a little time left to be here with me.

I took my mother home to die. Her family left, my father returned to his alcohol, and I felt alone. But I wasn't. God had been with me the entire time and loved me through the pain. God was not part of my home life, but when I was in middle school, I had been invited to church with a friend. I loved the acceptance and support I felt at church. The church became my extended family and surrounded me with the hands and feet of Jesus as my mother died.

The next few months were very difficult and I struggled terribly. Hospice was called in, but I was still with my mother 24/7. I was only 18 years old and this was not right! I should be planning my first semester at college, planning my future, not watching my mother be destroyed by an enemy called Glioplastoma. The tumor was like a spider web spreading in her brain, quickly taking her independence away, making her as helpless as a baby. The hardest thing was when her speech left. I would never hear my mother tell me "Brandi, I love you baby", or "I am so proud of you, Brandi" again.

As I was watching my mother slowly fade away, I found out I was pregnant. I wondered how I could take care of a child. I had no job, no car, and no money. What kind of future would my baby have? Everyone assumed I wanted to give the baby up for adoption, but I was so confused about the future. I felt I had the weight of the world on my shoulders, but then I started to feel the joy of my baby moving inside of me.

I had some family and church friends help, yet I felt alone. My mother was now totally bedridden. I was in complete despair. I wondered what I had done to deserve this. What had I done wrong? My mother started having grand mal seizures. I could only stand by as her body would thrust and shake uncontrollably in the bed, her mouth foaming, her eyes rolled back in her head. I remember sitting on the floor crying, wondering how I could handle all this. At this time, I felt a peace come over me and a desire to pray. I prayed and talked to Jesus all day and felt a calmness I had not felt before. I felt protected and guarded. As my mother slept I started to read the Bible each day. Every single day I was learning more and more of whom Jesus was, God was using this time to introduce Himself to me.

I started getting up early before my mother needed care. I would sit outside and watch the sun rise. I would hear the peace of His creation in the birds and the wind in the trees. As I got to know Jesus more, I started making changes in my life. I couldn't control much in my life but He started to teach me and show me the things in my life where I could choose His guidance. I learned to appreciate the simple things in life. God was teaching me that life is full of mountains, but if I held on to Him, He would take me through it. I learned to appreciate the ups and downs and realized there were always other people who had worse problems.

Things started to move quicker. My mother was getting worse and my belly was growing. I did not know how I was going to take care of a child. I felt Jesus wanted me to keep this child. I knew Jesus would take care of us somehow. I was alone with my mom when I went into labor. My baby was in distress and I needed an emergency C-section. My daughter is a miracle; the umbilical cord had been wrapped four times around her neck. She weighed only 3lbs 10oz. The doctors said she had not been getting nourishment for the past several weeks. I remember looking at her with love thinking that she is the closest thing to Jesus I could get. She was a reason to live, a reason to overcome the crazy life I was living.

On Father's Day, 1997, I woke up early and realized my mother had died in her sleep. In the silence of that morning I took time with my mother, to touch her, to look at her and cry out for losing her. I felt Jesus come and wrap me in His unbelievable warm embrace. He told me He loved me and would take care of me.

I was able to run to my church family who stood alongside me during the times to come by simply being the hands and feet of Jesus. They chose to allow God to live in and through them and I learned what being loved by Jesus felt like. I am now on the Care Team at my Church so that God can live in and through me to introduce someone who is hurting to His amazing grace and love. I am now able to use these painful experiences 17 years later to be the hands and feet of Jesus!

Brandi

My Story 39

"Let us then with confidence draw near to the throne of grace, that we may receive mercy and find grace to help in time of need"

Hebrews 4:16

It's All About Grace...

"Why Me God?"

Okay, so when bad things happen, disappointments come my way or I get sick or something, I really am not one to ask 'Why Me? Why not me? Who am I?' I'm no different than anyone else. I'm just as human as the next person.

When my son was murdered I did ask "Why Him?" The fact is, even if God came down here Himself and gave me an answer to that question it would not satisfy me. There are just those things in life that can't be understood this side of heaven!

So when do I ask; "Why Me God?" When it comes to God's grace, His divine grace, He shows me. I will see someone who is on the streets and obviously homeless, I think about my home and how fortunate I am and then I ask; "Why Me God?"

The more I learn and the more I seek God, the more I'm aware of how very little I truly understand. The more I learn, the less I know. I don't know why I was blessed with 2 beautiful boys and there are so many women who can't have a child. I don't know why I have a nice vehicle and so many have to walk or find transportation to where they need to go. Why did I survive cancer and others have died from it? So this is when I question 'Why Me God?'

I'm not special or any more deserving than the next person. I am no better nor am I any worse than anyone else. So why am I one of the 'haves' and not one of the 'have-nots'? I can assure you it's not because of anything I've done to deserve it. The only answer I have is grace, and I don't understand it! The answer doesn't necessarily make me feel any better; in fact I'm not sure how it makes me feel. It does however, bring me back to reality when I find myself in those times where I feel less than someone else or superior to another person. It puts me back in my place and reminds me that I am no one. We are all the same in the eyes of God.

What is grace? My husband and I were sharing thoughts on this the other night. It's been going through my mind since. So I decided to do some spiritual investigation. I started by looking up the definition of grace. This is what I found: 1) the exercise of love, kindness, mercy, favor; disposition to benefit or serve another; favor bestowed or privilege conferred. 2) The divine favor toward man; the mercy of God distinguished from His justice alone; divine love or pardon; a state of acceptance with God.

Well that gives me a good starting place but it also makes me scream even louder, "Why me?!" Grace is a gift. I can't earn it, I can't buy it, and there is nothing I can do to receive it except believe in it. For me that means believing in God and believing that His son died for my sins. He died for all of us; that's grace. None of us deserve forgiveness or eternal life, but we are all welcome to accept this free gift bestowed on us by the Almighty Father, God. It's all about grace.

Although I can't do anything to acquire grace, I do feel like there is a responsibility on my part where grace is concerned. I need to develop an attitude of gratitude and a thankful spirit is essential. This brings me to the 1st definition where it talks about disposition to benefit or serve another. Words like love, kindness and mercy are associated with grace. It seems to me, that to be thankful for the grace that I've been given is about showing my gratitude. I need to share this grace with others. Perhaps grace is a lesson from the Lord. He is teaching us to 'Pay it Forward'.

Lynda

Conclusion

> *"Blessed is the man who perseveres under trial, because when he has stood the test, he will receive the crown of life that God has promised to those who love Him"*
>
> James 1:12

Life can be difficult for us all. By saying you are a Christ follower, does not protect you from the pain of the sin in this world. But saying you are a Christ follower; you are allowing Christ to help you through the fires of life. He cares about what you are going through, the day to day trials, whether small or extreme.

When I was at my low point, I felt too weak for faith. My slogan was; "I am hanging on the ankles of Jesus, so He could drag me through the day." A very good visual I thought! But a good friend pointed out how wrong that was. Jesus always wants to carry me, to let me rest on Him. The visual of resting my head on the shoulders of Jesus Christ, as he carries me through, is a much sweeter thought.

I pray you will learn to rest on Him, let Jesus Christ carry you during your trial, to put your tired head against His chest and let Him take you to through the fire.

Blessings

Do you have your own story to tell? Did one of these stories touch your heart? Please share on the blog at www.MyStoryYourStory2.com

About the Author

"Praise be to the God and Father of our Lord Jesus Christ, the Father of compassion and the God of all comfort, who comforts us in all our troubles, so that we can comfort those in any trouble with the comfort we ourselves have received from God. For just as the sufferings of Christ flow over into our lives, so also through Christ our comfort overflows."

2 Corinthians 1:3-5

Throughout my life, I have been hit by the pain and difficulties of life. I didn't always feel the comfort of Christ overflowing in my suffering. I have felt more alone at times than filled with the peace of knowing that Jesus was with me.

How could life be so hard and painful? Where is God during this trial? What good can come from this?

"If we are distressed, it is for your comfort and salvation; if we are comforted, it is for your comfort, which produces in you a patient endurance of the same sufferings we suffer. And our hope for you is firm, because we know that just as you share in our sufferings, so also you share in our comfort."

2 Corinthians 1: 6-7

Yet, as I looked and found peace and comfort in God's Word, I am now able to give praise, glory, and honor because Jesus Christ was revealed in those trials. I know that by His glory I have endured this life and can share and comfort others in their suffering. I have learned that He will be with me always.

Subject Index

The trials written in these devotionals bring out many different emotions. This subject index may help to find the story similar to the trial you may be going through now. (The reference numbers listed are the *MyStory* number, not page numbers).

Abuse: 1, 8, 12, 15, 17, 19, 20, 23
Acceptance: 2, 3, 4, 5, 7, 10, 11, 12, 13, 17, 20, 21, 25, 27, 28, 30, 34, 35, 38
Addiction: 11, 14, 24, 38
Anger: 1, 5, 7, 11, 12, 16, 17, 20, 23, 25, 35, 38
Assurance/Encouragement: 2, 4, 10, 15, 17, 22, 28, 30, 38, 39
Betrayal: 1, 5, 12, 15, 17, 19, 23, 31, 32, 38
Cancer: 4, 7, 8, 38
Courage/Strength: 3, 4, 9, 10, 11, 12, 13, 15, 17, 22, 26, 28, 32, 38
Cystic Fibrosis: 2, 13, 16, 33, 35
Darkness/Hopelessness: 5, 12, 14, 15, 16, 18, 21, 24, 25, 29, 38
Death 2, 17, 18, 19, 22, 24, 29, 35, 38
Depression: 5, 6, 14, 15, 16, 19, 21, 33

Divorce/Infidelity: 1, 3, 5, 12, 28, 32, 35, 38
Doubt: 3, 4, 6, 7, 12, 13, 15, 16, 20, 21, 25
Fear: 7, 9, 12, 13, 15, 17, 18, 19, 20, 23, 28, 33, 38
Glioblastoma: 38
Grace: 6, 8, 10, 11, 12, 14, 15, 17, 27, 32, 38, 39
Grief: 2, 5, 7, 15, 25, 22, 29, 31, 38
Heart pain: 7, 12, 13, 14, 15, 19, 22, 23, 24, 28, 29, 32, 33, 36, 38
Hope: 3, 4, 7, 8, 9, 12, 14, 15, 17, 22, 23, 24, 26, 29, 30, 38, 39
Illness: 2, 4, 7, 8, 10, 13, 14, 22, 25, 28, 30, 36, 37, 38
Infertility: 7, 29
Isolation/Loneliness: 5, 6, 10, 12, 13, 15, 16, 21, 22, 23, 31, 35, 36, 38

Joy: 8, 10, 22, 26, 28, 30, 31, 36
Lyme disease: 25, 30
Multiple Sclerosis: 37
Peace: 2, 4, 7, 12, 11, 13, 15, 19, 21,
    22, 24, 27, 28, 31, 37, 38, 39
PTSD: 9, 15, 19, 23
Rape: 15, 19
Relationship issues: 1, 5, 12, 15,
    17, 23, 28, 32, 35

Sexual Desires: 11, 24
Trust (loss of): 1, 4, 7, 12, 13, 15,
    16, 17, 18, 23, 28, 30
Victim: 1, 8, 12, 14, 15, 17, 19,
    23, 35
Worry: 4, 7, 9, 18, 23, 30, 38